W9-AYR-696

DATE DUE			

Son

4f

GAYLORD M2G

Berkley Books by Jack Maguire

THE HALLOWEEN BOOK
THE CHRISTMAS BOOK

THE
CHRISTMAS
BOOK

JACK MAGUIRE

Produced by The Philip Lief Group, Inc.

Illustrations by Tamara Dubin Brown

B

BERKLEY BOOKS, NEW YORK 6237911

THE CHRISTMAS BOOK

A Berkley Book / published by arrangement with
The Philip Lief Group, Inc.

PRINTING HISTORY
Berkley edition / November 1994

ISBN: 0-425-14510-7

BERKLEY®
Berkley Books are published by The Berkley Publishing Group,
200 Madison Avenue, New York, New York 10016.
BERKLEY and the "B" design
are trademarks belonging to Berkley Publishing Corporation.

PRINTED IN THE UNITED STATES OF AMERICA

10 9 8 7 6 5 4 3 2 1

CONTENTS

⚔ ⚔ ⚔

CHAPTER 1

⧋⧋⧋

The Christmas Tree

According to legend, Martin Luther, the sixteenth-century Reformationist, is personally responsible for the Christmas tree as we know it today. The story says that he was trudging home through the woods after a Christmas Eve sermon when he was suddenly struck by the beauty of a towering pine tree. It stretched toward heaven like a living steeple; the stars shining through it appeared to be hanging from its branches; and its fragrance stirred his soul far more than the finest incense ever had. Determined to share the wonder of this experience with his family, he cut down a smaller pine tree nearby, brought it home, and set it up in the front room, with candles in its branches to represent the stars.

Whether or not Luther actually did create the first official Christmas tree, the practice of decorating an evergreen tree to celebrate a wintertime holiday goes

1

back at least 4,000 years, when the Babylonians trimmed cedars to honor Marduk, their sun god, on the winter solstice. From the Middle East, the solstice-tree tradition spread throughout the Mediterranean and Northern Europe. The Romans erected cut evergreens to celebrate Saturnalia, and the Celts and the Teutons bedecked live evergreens to commemorate the turning of winter to spring. Thus, the modern Christmas tree has a heritage that goes back as far as recorded history itself.

Creating a special tree to be the focal point of your holiday celebration is an act of love. It honors the vital connection of each human being to the natural world as well as to the spiritual world. And it affirms the everlasting impulse of life toward joy, beauty, and sharing.

Tree Safety

If you're buying a cut tree, choose the freshest tree possible. To allow for better water conduction, cut an inch off the trunk just before mounting the tree in its stand and water immediately. If you're not mounting the tree as soon as you bring it home, cut an inch off the trunk just before sitting the tree in a bucket of water. (For guidelines on determining a tree's freshness, see "Cut Trees: Selecting, Tending, and Afterward" in this chapter.)

Use a tree stand that holds at least one gallon of water.

Make sure a smoke detector is installed somewhere near the tree. Special dectectors that can be clipped right onto the tree are available from a number of sources, including Companion Products (call 800-521-0505). Also, make sure that a fire extinguisher, recently checked, is easily accessible, and that everyone in your household knows how to use it.

Keep the tree away from traffic paths, drafts such as windows that are occasionally opened, and heat sources such as fireplaces, radiators, and television sets.

Always use lights with "UL" (Underwriters Laboratories) indicated on the label. Never use lighted candles, either on or near the tree.

Check and replace worn or damaged light sets or wires.

Avoid "octopus" connections and too many lead cords, which can overload circuits.

Avoid playing with electrically operated toys directly under the tree.

If you want to decorate your tree with spray-on flocking and angel hair, make sure to spray the tree first, then add the angel hair. Neither the flocking nor the angel hair is combustile by itself or when combined in the manner just stated, but snow sprayed on top of angel hair is very combustible.

To prevent young children and pets from inadvertently injuring themselves, hang unbreakable ornaments with no sharp edges, small parts, or overly enticing features on the lower branches, and decorate these branches somewhat sparingly. Save flashier, more fragile, and more complex ornaments for the upper branches.

If someone drops a glass ornament and it shatters, pick up the pieces by gently pressing a wadded and dampened paper towel on top of them. Don't attempt to pick them up with your fingers.

Check live trees and cut trees daily to make sure they are getting enough water: The average cut tree needs about one quart of water daily per one inch of trunk diameter. Remove the tree from your home as soon as it has dried out.

To keep young children or pets from tipping over the tree, use wire or a nylon cord (such as fishing line) to secure the trunk of the tree to the wall(s) or ceiling.

Remove discarded wrappings and packages from the tree area as soon as possible.

Do not leave tree lights on when no one is at home or when no one is awake at home.

Make sure that the fire department number is posted in a conspicuous place near the telephone and that all members of your household know what to do in case of a fire-related emergency.

Varieties of Natural Christmas Trees

Balsam Fir

The balsam fir has short, flat, dark green needles that are usually rounded at the tip and hold well to their twigs. The needles arranged on their twigs closely resemble feathers, and the twigs themselves generally grow at right angles to their respective branches. Greenish brown, rounded bud tips are coated with a waxy pitch, and the bark is gray or brown, thin, and smooth. The tree as a whole offers relatively generous space between branches for ornaments.

Balsam Fir

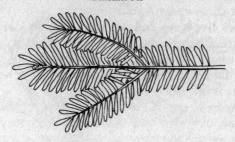

Douglas Fir

Like the balsam fir, the Douglas fir has dark green needles arranged like feathers on their twigs, but the needles are somewhat longer. The needles hold well; in fact, many needles hold to their twigs even after they've browned. Instead of greenish brown, rounded buds, like the balsam fir, the Douglas fir has reddish brown buds that narrow at the tip into a sharp point.

Douglas Fir

Scotch Pine

The Scotch pine has significantly longer needles than the balsam or Douglas firs. The needles grow in clusters of two, often have a gray green or blue green tint,

Scotch Pine

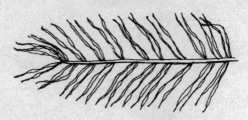

and are slightly twisted. They hold to their twigs better than almost any other evergreen. The bark is scaly and orange red in hue.

White Pine

White Pine
The white pine features bundles of soft, thin needles that have a gray green or silvery green cast. They hold well but get brittle fairly rapidly. There are two major types of white pine: Eastern and Western. The Eastern type has much longer and thinner needles.

Norway Spruce
The needles of the Norway spruce are dark green, four-sided, stiff, and sharp. The tree is densely

Norway Spruce

packed with branches that dip and sweep gracefully, and the needle retention is good, but not as good as a pine or a fir.

Blue Spruce

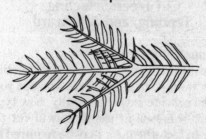

Blue Spruce
The needles of the blue spruce have a beautiful and distinctive blue green to blue gray cast, and they are somewhat more compact on their branches than the needles of the Norway spruce. Otherwise the two trees are very similar.

Red Cedar

Red Cedar

A tree common in the eastern United States, the red
cedar is easy to spot because of its extremely short,
dark green, scalelike needles (actually, the needles
look more like tiny leaves). The tree is attractive, but
sheds needles faster than most other evergreens.

Cut Trees: Selecting,
Tending, and Afterward

Cutting Your Own Tree

For the freshest tree possible and a fun holiday ad-
venture as well, go to a tree farm and cut your own
tree. Farms provide saws (generally, bow type) but,
if you want, someone at the farm will cut the tree
you select. In fact, the farm may be required by local
laws to cut trees for its patrons rather than letting
patrons cut their own.

Farm tree prices and varieties are normally com-
parable to street tree prices and varieties, but the
farm trees last for a much longer time. Many farms
allow you to come in advance—usually anytime after
Thanksgiving—to select and reserve your tree.

When visiting farms, dress warmly with boots and gloves, and bring twine to tie the tree to your car roof or to tie the trunk closed. It's also a good idea to bring a measure or lengths of string cut to suit your tree height and width preference: Trees outdoors tend to look smaller than they do indoors. Also, be sure to call ahead to check directions, weather conditions, times of operation, prices, and procedures.

Always go to a tree farm for cutting a tree, rather than cutting a tree from open woods. The trees growing on tree farms are systematically replenished and, while they perform significant environmental services such as adding oxgen to the air and filtering airborne pollutants, they are not performing vital roles in the ecological system, such as providing homes and ground cover for animals or helping to control erosion. The same things cannot be said of trees in the open woods. Cutting down the latter type of tree can be very damaging from an ecological point of view.

Buying a Street Tree

Here are guidelines for buying a tree that's already been cut (commonly called a "street tree," though it can be sold in a store, on a lot, from the back of a truck, or even on board a boat).

Decide in advance what size and type of tree you want. Above all, avoid buying a tree that is too tall or too full for its intended location in your home. With this in mind, you may want to take along a measure or lengths of string cut to suit your tree height and girth preferences.

Research your area for "rent-a-tree" possibilities. Here's how a rent-a-tree program works: An organization charges a minimal fee for the tree itself plus a deposit fee. If the tree is returned by a certain deadline after the Christmas season, renters get their deposit back. The tree is then recycled by the organization, usually as mulch.

One such organization in the New York City area is IKEA, a home furnishing chain. In 1992, for example, IKEA rented 35,000 six to ten-foot Douglas fir trees for a flat rate of $10 per tree, plus a $10 deposit (trees were due back by January 10, 1993). IKEA even gave renters a special bonus: a coupon for a free blue spruce sapling redeemable the following spring.

Wear gloves to make carrying the cut tree more comfortable. Also, take along some twine to tie the tree to the roof of your car, to tie the trunk lid shut, or to bale your tree so that it's slimmer for transport.

Take someone with you to shop. One person can hold the tree while the other steps back to evaluate it more accurately.

To check for good symmetry, rotate each tree that you're considering. You may be able to accept a tree that has a "bad" side if you plan to put it into an area such as the corner of a room. Such a tree may even be desirable, since it will take up less floor space in your home. However, the ideal tree symmetry is as follows.

- The width of the lowest branches should measure about one half to two-thirds of the tree's height.
- There should be no spots noticeably empty of branches.
- The tree should be shaped as closely as possible to a cone, tapering about forty-five to sixty de-

grees from the top down (or trimmable to such a shape).

If you can't find the ideal tree, bear in mind that it may be possible to fill in open spaces in a tree by trimming or removing unwanted branches and inserting them into holes drilled into the trunk. You also may be able to camouflage open spots by tying surrounding branches into new positions, using black nylon thread attached first to the middle of the branch, and then to the trunk of the tree or to the middle of another branch that is very sturdy.

Check the tree to make sure the trunk is straight, especially at the bottom, so that the tree won't be crooked when it's mounted in its stand. Also make sure that the trunk is not thicker than the opening of your stand.

Sniff to see if the tree has a strong fragrance. This may or may not be a sign of freshness, but it certainly adds to the tree's ambiance. Make sure the interior needles are not brown.

To test the needles for freshness and retention, try bending a single needle from the tip with your index finger. If it breaks instead of bending, it's brittle. Then try running your finger down a branch to see if many needles fall off. Finally, grasp the tree by the trunk and lightly bang it on the ground to see if many needles shower down. You should expect a certain degree of needle brittleness and needle shedding, but it should be minimal or else the tree won't last long in your home.

Spreading your forearm across random groups of branches, bear down gently to see if the branches are strong and how they will drape with the weight of the ornaments. Sometimes the branches of a street tree will be packed unnaturally tightly due to having been baled for transport. Bear in mind that such trees will take up more room and have a more "open" look later, in your home.

If you know you're going to be mounting the tree in its stand within a couple of hours, and you don't want to be bothered with cutting the trunk yourself, ask the tree-seller to cut it for you. An inch off the trunk, eliminating any resinous seal there, is all you need to help the tree absorb water more easily, but you may want to cut off more to accommodate your tree stand and to trim the tree to the height you desire.

Tending the Tree at Home
Here are guidelines for setting up and taking care of your cut tree at home (also see "Tree Safety" in this chapter, and Chapter 2, "Trimming the Tree").

If possible, store the tree for the first day in a sheltered, unheated area, such as a porch, garage, or basement, with the tree stem soaking in a bucket of water. This will allow the tree to adjust gradually to indoor temperatures, thus ensuring better needle retention. Also, be sure to remove any baling strings as soon as you've brought the tree home. This will give the branches time to settle to their proper positions before you begin decorating. If it's not possible to allow for unheated storage, try to wait at least twelve hours after mounting the tree in its stand before decorating it. This gives the tree time to settle in its new position.

Inside your home, choose a cool, highly visible spot for your tree that's close to one or more electrical outlets. You may also want to consider positioning your tree near a window so that it can be viewed from outside. Just be certain that the tree won't be subjected to drafts.

In addition to filling the tree stand with water, lightly sprinkle or spray water on the branches and needles. Then allow about a half hour for the tree to dry before decorating it. This, too, will help needle retention.

Take care not to let the water level in the stand drop below the end of the tree stem, or a resinous seal will begin to form. Many so-called "tree tea" concoctions, to be added to the tree water, claim to prolong needle retention, but none has yet been proven to work.

The following chart indicates the approximate number of decorations a tree can comfortably and attractively support, based on its height.

HEIGHT	MINI-LIGHTS	GARLANDS	ORNAMENTS
3'	250	25'	50
4'	350	40'	75
5'	400	55'	100
6'	450	75'	150
7'	550	90'	200
8'	700	110'	275

Afterward

Here are guidelines for disposing of your tree when the holiday season is over (January 6, Twelfth Night, is the traditional last day).

After removing all decorations and lights, wrap the tree in a sheet or tarp to remove it from the home. This will minimize fallen-needle mess.

Call your local government's sanitation department to inquire about or confirm tree disposal rules and procedures.

Consider recycling the tree or parts of the tree yourself, in one or more of the following manners.

- Create an instant feeding and nesting station for birds. "Plant" or lay the tree outdoors on your property in a relatively secure and secluded spot, and festoon it with orange slices, suet, bread, popcorn, and peanut butter mixed with birdseed.
- Sink the tree into your own fish pond, or (with permission) some other private fish pond, where it will make an excellent feeding and refuge area for fish.
- Chop up the tree and use it as mulch in a garden, border, walkway, or animal stall. Whole branches also work well as wintertime mulch or weather shields, provided they are firmly anchored into the ground or against a barrier such as the sides of a tree guard, wooden tub, or window box.
- Cut off branch tips and use them as fragrance enhancers in simmering potpourris and aromatic sachets. Balsam needles retain their scent indefinitely if stored in a brown paper bag.
- Shear the trunk and use sections of the wood for woodworking projects such as making candlesticks, paperweights, and birdhouses; or use the entire trunk to edge a walkway or garden.
- Shear the the trunk and store it in a garage, attic, or basement; the following Christmas season, use it (or a section of it) as a Yule log. Historically, the Teutons practiced this form of recycling, also using the same sheared trunk on May Day, as a Maypole.

To cut up or shear a tree, pruning shears work much better than a saw or scissors. Wear heavy gloves throughout the process, and confine the tree to a large plastic sheet to avoid needle and sap mess.

Research your area for organizations that accept discarded trees for use as mulch or erosion barriers (the latter use is especially prevalent at beaches). Start by contacting your local department of public works for information.

Guidelines for Buying and Using an Artifical Tree

Artificial trees come in many varieties, so shop around carefully to get exactly the tree you want. Generally speaking, there are two major types: soft needle (needles are about 4" long, with a featherlike appearance) and hard needle (needles are 1–2" long, with a crisp, furlike appearance). However, within each of these two broad types are many variations. Some closely resemble natural evergreens such as balsam fir, Douglas fir, and Scotch pine; others have a more exotic look all their own.

Better quality artificial trees tend to employ different shades of green, with perhaps a hint of blue or gray on the needles to give the overall tree a more natural look. Some of these artificial trees even have realistic-looking buds on the tips of their branches. In addition, better quality trees tend to have downswept branches, rather than upswept or outswept branches. As the name implies, downswept branches arch slightly toward ground level from the trunk, giving the tree a fuller look.

One kind of artificial tree that has been rapidly

gaining popularity in recent years is the goose-feather tree. Making no pretense to pass as a real tree, the goose-feather tree nevertheless evokes the spirit of a Christmas tree with a great deal of folk art charm.

Historians claim that the goose-feather tree orginated in Germany in the mid-nineteenth century, when concern about dwindling pine forests led to

Goose-Feather-Tree

stricter laws about cutting down pines for Christmas trees. Early varieties featured actual goose feathers as branches, which were stuck into a wooden pole; but today's trees are fashioned from many different kinds of feathers or featherlike substitutes made from natural materials. These trees are relatively small, usually ranging from one to three feet tall, so they are especially good at lending a stylish holiday touch to a hallway or tabletop.

Aside from aesthetic considerations in selecting an artificial Christmas tree, there are also safety considerations. Despite any claim to the contrary, no artificial tree is fireproof unless it's made entirely of unpainted metal. Nevertheless, artificial trees can and should be flame retardant, which means they will be more inclined to melt or char rather than burn. Look for a label specifically stating that the tree is flame retardant.

When decorating your artificial tree, bear in mind that strings of electric lights can be even more hazardous on artificial trees than they are on real trees. Use only miniature bulbs, not large ones. Avoid ceramic-coated or translucent bulbs. Give strong consideration to light alternatives other than strings of bulbs: Direct a spotlight on the tree, or decorate the tree with "optic sprays," which are tiny hairlike strands that pick up light from a source below the tree.

The Live Tree Alternative

An ancient Teuton would celebrate the winter solstice by moving a live tree—roots and all—to an inside tub, using it as a centerpiece during the holiday season, and then replanting it outside after the season was over. Many Americans are reviving this custom.

The motivation for choosing a live tree is not just environmental awareness. After all, supporting a tree farm by buying a street tree or cutting one's own tree also helps the environment (it may even be more helpful, at least on a global level, since the average tree farm plants two seedlings for every tree cut). An equally strong motivation for choosing a live tree is the two-for-one thrill of having an indoor tree for Christmas that turns into an outdoor tree afterward, improving the property and recalling the Christmas spirit all year long, year after year.

Like many good things, however, a live tree does not come easy. Selecting, preserving, and transplanting a live tree requires careful planning and a certain amount of plain old hard work. If you'd like to have a live tree, follow these steps.

Dig the tree hole before you buy the tree, and before the ground is likely to freeze. In many parts of the country, the ground can freeze during the Christmas season, making post-season digging extremely difficult. At any rate, you probably won't feel much like digging the hole after Christmas.

If you are uncertain when to expect the ground to freeze in your area, ask a local nursery or weather service. In some areas of the country, freezing may start as early as November and may continue unpredictably throughout December and January, so you might want to dig your hole as early as late October.

Before you dig your hole, decide on the style and size of the tree you want to buy. Ask a local nursery to recommend trees that grow well in your area and to estimate prices and root ball sizes for different styles and sizes of trees.

Also before you dig, test your soil for drainage. You can do this by digging a hole about a foot deep where you intend to plant and then filling the hole with water. If the water doesn't drain away completely in

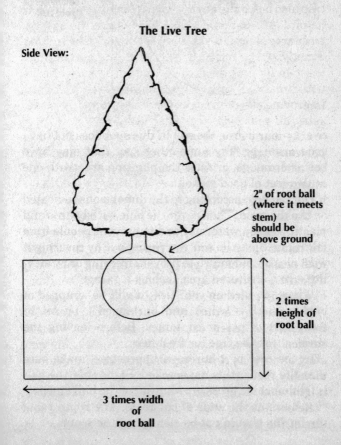

The Live Tree

Side View:

2" of root ball (where it meets stem) should be above ground

2 times height of root ball

3 times width of root ball

Top View:

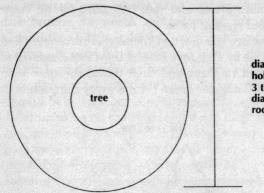

tree

diameter of
hole circle=
3 times
diameter of
root ball

Tree

twenty-four hours, the soil in this spot does not have
good drainage. Try some other spot that may have
better drainage, or raise the planting area with one
or two feet of good topsoil.

Dig the hole according to the dimensions indicated
on the diagram. Then cover the hole with boards and
plastic to keep water out and to prevent people from
falling in. Save the soil you've dug out by covering it
with plastic and mulch to prevent freezing or by moving it to a sheltered area such as a garage.

When you pick up your tree, it will be wrapped in
burlap (B&B—"balled and burlapped"), or set in
some sort of pot or container. Before leaving the
store, check the tree for freshness.

In the case of a burlap-wrapped tree, make sure
that the root ball is not cracked. Signs that the ball
is fresh include grass growing out of the ball and new
root hairs at the ends of cut roots. The ropes tying
the burlap should not be strangling the roots.

In the case of a potted tree, make sure that the soil feels moist and that roots are not growing out of the pot from the top or bottom. Also poke around with your index finger from the edge of the container in toward the center. Some nurseries base the price of potted trees on the size of the container; if there's more than a couple of inches of soil between the container edge and the root ball, you may wind up paying more than the true size of the tree warrants.

If you plan to store the tree for a while before setting it up inside, be sure to store it in a sheltered, unheated place like a porch or garage where it will not be subject to freezing. Keep the root ball watered, but avoid soaking it.

For best results, once the tree is moved indoors, it shouldn't remain there longer than seven days. Otherwise, the warmth of the house may cause it to break dormancy and begin its growth cycle, making it too vulnerable to withstand wintertime planting. With this in mind, choose an indoor spot for the tree that is relatively cool.

Make sure that the tree is secure in its tub and that the tub allows for tree watering (if the tub is not metal or plastic, wrap the root ball in plastic). Keep the root ball slightly moist, but not flooded.

Decorate the tree sparingly, with care. If strings of electric lights are used, they must not give off heat, and you must not mist the tree.

Do not remove the tree directly from the house to the outdoors. Instead, move it to a sheltered, unheated place for several days so that it can gradually adjust to the change in temperature.

When it's time to plant the tree, do not remove any burlap around the root ball. Do remove any plastic.

Sometimes a plastic burlap is used on root balls. If the burlap is, in fact, plastic, it should be removed. Keep as much of the original soil around the root ball as possible. Plant the tree with the soil you dug out of the hole, according to the diagram.

Do not add fertilizer, compost, or peat moss to the planting soil, or the roots may not grow beyond the original hole. Avoid tamping the soil until the hole is about two-thirds full, and then tamp very gently every now and then as you continue to fill the hole to the top. Cover the soil directly over the root ball with 2–3" of mulch. Leave the rest of the soil un-mulched to avoid creating a nesting area for insects, fungus, or rodents.

Give the tree a slow, deep watering during any week that has not received at least ½" of precipita-tion (rain or snow), as long as the ground isn't com-pletely frozen. Keep a tin can with a measuring line near the tree to gauge the weekly precipitation. Con-tinue this practice for the first two years that the tree is outdoors.

CHAPTER 2

♣♣♣

Trimming the Tree

Christmas tree ornaments used to be very limited in variety, dictated by tradition. The earliest known Christmas tree decorations, dating from around 1600 in Germany, consisted of round sugar cookies (meant to symbolize Communion wafers), apples (artificial or dried, meant to symbolize the apples in Paradise), and paper roses in many different colors (roses are associated with the Virgin Mary). Wealthy households often added gold foil cutouts or streamers to this traditional ornamentation scheme. Candles weren't common on Christmas trees until about a century later, when other varieties of ornaments, many of which doubled as small gifts, also began appearing on trees throughout Germany and Scandinavia.

Today, anything goes as far as Christmas tree decorations are concerned. Ornaments might be glass balls, candy canes, and noisemakers, or blinking disco lights, starship models, and battery-operated action figures. Dazed by such a multitude of different types of ornaments from which to choose, many people like to establish a particular theme for their tree, one that they keep from year to year. Other tree decorators take a more eclectic approach, deliberately choosing to bedazzle the senses with a wide variety of ornament types. Still others attempt a sort of compromise, switching themes from year to year.

Regardless of your particular tree trimming style, you'll be attracted to the eye-catching ideas in this chapter. Included are suggestions for giving your tree a theme, and instructions for making your own ornaments—whether or not your tree has a theme.

Christmas Tree Themes

To some degree, all decorated Christmas trees, regardless of the decorators' intentions, turn out to be theme trees. They inevitably wind up reflecting the special interests or tastes of their decorators. A consciously crafted theme tree, however, can add a very special dimension to Christmas, evoking a particular world of beauty that has personal significance.

If you prefer to decorate your Christmas tree each year with the same crazy but lovable mix of ornaments that you've always used, why not have a second, smaller tree in another room that you can decorate as a theme tree, perhaps varying the theme from year to year? Experiment with ornaments that reflect different hobbies or different ethnic themes, or try some of the suggestions offered below.

1. *Santa Claus.* In addition to figures of Santa in the form of cookies, cutouts, and three-dimensional ornaments, include figures of elves, toys, reindeer, sleighs, stockings, and pipes. You can also decorate the tree with jingle bells (singly, on ribbons, or in chains) and candy canes.

2. *Nature.* Decorate the tree with animal-related ornaments (preferably naturalistic). You can also include pinecones, fruits (real or artifical), seashells, starfish, pieces of driftwood, and strings of berries.

3. *Needlepoint.* Consisting mainly of needlepoint ornmanents, this tree can also include other needlework pieces such as lace, crotchet, quilting, and stitchery (see "Stitched Star" in this section). You can add brightly colored ribbons or ropes of yarn.

4. *Dolls.* Most of your ornaments should be miniature dolls, but you can also use fabric or sequin-covered balls (see "Decorated Balls" in this section), pieces of costume jewelry, and figures of gloves, umbrellas, and fancy boots. Supplement these ornaments with ropes of beads.

5. *Country.* The country look can be achieved by using cookies or cookie cutters, simple wooden figures like moons and stars, paper cutouts (see "Twin Hearts" in this section), raffia bows, doily snowflakes, tiny stuffed animals, and strings of popcorn.

6. *Nutcracker*. Taking its cue from the classic Tchaikovsky ballet that's so closely associated with the Christmas season, this tree can feature figures of ballet dancers, mice, Russian-style nutcracker soldiers, and orchestral instruments. It can also be decked with ballet slippers, velvet balls (see "Decorated Balls" in this section), silk flowers, lace-and-ribbon ornaments, sugared fruits (real or artificial), and nuts (real or artifical, gilded or plain).

7. *Victorian*. Popular ornaments during the Victorian era in England and America were folded paper fans, baskets of foil-wrapped candy, cornucopias (see "Cornucopias" in this section), small flags, paper valentines (or similarly ornate paper cutouts), nosegays, toy soldiers, and gold ribbons.

8. *Fiction and Fantasy*. In addition to featuring cutouts and figurines of Christmas characters like Santa and Frosty the Snowman, you can also include your favorite characters from stories, poems, films, television, and folklore, such as Pinocchio, the Cowardly Lion, Cinderella, Pooh, Raggedy Ann, Puss-in-Boots, Snoopy, Wile E. Coyote, and Superman. Other possible ornaments include miniature books, scrolls, quills, pens, motion picture cameras, or small pages with favorite quotes.

9. *Homemade*. Trim the entire tree with decorations made by hand. Include both purchased

craft ornaments such as whittled figurines, origami, or tin cutouts and ornaments made in your own home (see all the homemade ornament suggestions in this section of the book).

10. *Angel*. As the basis of this tree scheme, use a lot of angel ornaments. Add figures of harps, stars, the sun, and the moon. Drape the boughs with angel hair or ropes of gold and silver tinsel.

11. *Food*. In addition to lots of candies and cookies— especially clusters of gumdrops, sugar cookies, and gingerbread people—decorate the tree with fruit (real or artifical), candy canes, toy cooking utensils, cookie cutters, paper doilies, and chains of popcorn and cranberries (also, see "Baker's Clay" in this section).

12. *Outdoor Fun*. For an adventurous Northern wilderness look, decorate the tree with figures of sleds, snowshoes, skates, skis, hockey sticks, canoes, reindeer, bears, fish, and ducks. Spray or coat the boughs with artifical snow.

13. *Color*. Choose a color scheme such as gold, red and green, black and white, or purple, teal, and silver, and carry out that scheme in all the ornamentation.

14. *Toys*. Decorate the tree with ornaments suggesting toys, such as toy soldiers, dolls, teddy bears, musical instruments, blocks, and balls (see "Decorated Balls" in this section). Add tiny

wrapped packages, candy canes, and ribbon bows.

15. *Flowers*. In addition to ornaments suggesting flowers, deck the tree with dried flowers, gold-painted and silver-painted fruits and seed pods, sprigs of mistletoe or holly, and strings of berries.

Paper Chains

Paper chains are showy, easy to make, and conjure delightful memories of childhood. The standard way to make paper chains is to link one rectangular strip of construction paper around another, forming a chain of rings. For a more intricate, sophisticated look, try this Swedish-style variation. You need:

- Construction paper: numerous 6" × 12" sheets in assorted colors
- Pair of scissors

Directions for making paper chains:

1. Fold one sheet of construction paper in half, forming a square. Then fold the square in half by bending the folded side of the square.

2. Cut the folded 3" × 6" rectangle according to the pattern shown. The result will be one link in the chain.

Paper Chain

1.

Fold 1

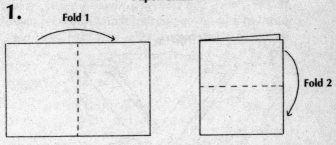

Fold 2

2.

3. On one side of the link, fold the four "legs" so that they stick out. On the other side of the link, fold the other four legs so that they stick out in the opposite direction.

3.

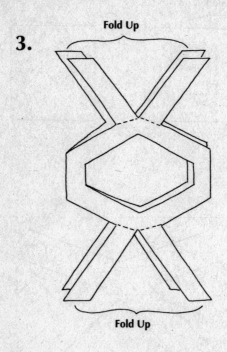

Fold Up

Fold Up

4. Using another sheet of construction paper with a pleasantly contrasting color, cut another link, following steps 1 and 2 above. Then proceed to step 5 before performing step 3.

4.

5. Join one link to another by slipping the new open link through the previous closed link. To make the new link fit through, you will need to bend it carefully down the middle, so that you can easily flatten it back once it's through.

Stitched Star

1.

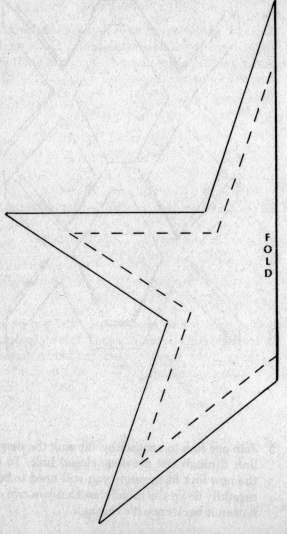

F
O
L
D

Actual-Size Pattern

Stitched Star

The star shape is versatile and eye-catching, especially in a three-dimensional format. However, if you prefer another shape, simply substitute another pattern and follow the directions for making the stitched star.

You need:

- Two 5" × 5" pieces of white muslin
- Scraps of fabric in assorted colors
- Scissors
- Needle and white thread
- Cotton batting (or similar stuffing material)

Directions for making the stitched star:

1. Cut two star-shaped pieces of white muslin according to the pattern shown (which leaves a ¼" seam all around the star).

2. For each white muslin star, cut six or seven smaller stars from assorted fabric scraps. Arrange these smaller stars randomly across the outward-facing side of each muslin star, taking care not to cover the seam. Stitch each smaller star in place.

2.

Actual-Size Pattern

3. Stitch the two muslin stars together along the seam, leaving the entire top point open for stuffing.

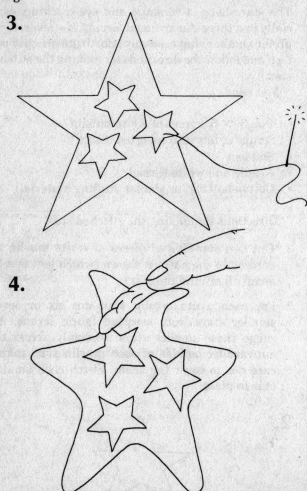

3.

4.

4. Stuff the star with cotton batting, then slip-stitch the open point.

5. From the leftover muslin, cut a small, slim rectangle that can be folded for a hanging loop. Stitch this loop to the tip of the stuffed star's top point.

Decorated Balls

Christmas tree balls derive from the apples that were traditionally hung on early Christmas trees to symbolize the apples of Paradise (Paradise having been symbolically regained for humankind through Christ). Red remains the most popular color for Christmas tree balls, but any resemblance to an apple usually stops there.

For decorated balls, you need:

- Styrofoam balls (available in art supply stores in various sizes)
- Assorted lengths of fabric (in pleasantly contrasting colors or patterns)
- A generous supply of sequins, beads, and straight pins
- Pipe cleaners

Directions for making decorated balls:

1. From assorted fabrics, cut six pieces on the bias, according to the pattern shown (a ball 5" in diameter requires pieces that are 7" tall).

Decorated Balls

2. On the surface of the ball, pin the the six fabric pieces next to each other, with edges slightly overlapping, so that they cover the entire surface. Use just enough pins to keep the pieces in place. More secure pinning will come later, in step 4.

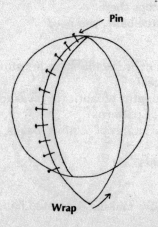

3.

3. At the top of the ball, where the six fabric pieces meet, insert a pipe cleaner halfway into the ball. Bend it to form a hanging hook.

4. All along the pinned seams of the six fabric pieces, pin alternating sequins and beads in attractive colors.

4.

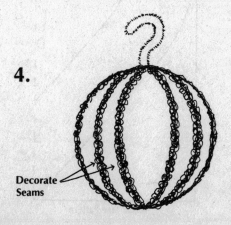

Decorate Seams

Twin Hearts

Twin hearts are traditional Christmas tree decorations in Scandinavia, but their appeal is universal.

You need:

- Sheets of red construction paper
- Green yarn
- Scissors
- Glue (all-purpose)

Twin Hearts

1.

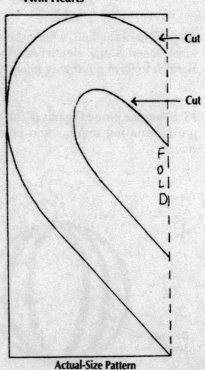

Actual-Size Pattern

Directions for making twin hearts:

1. Using the red construction paper, cut five hearts of equal size, based on squares that are 3½" × 3½".

2. From the center of each of these five hearts, cut out a heart that is 2" × 2". To do this, begin by folding the larger heart vertically in half (according to the illustration). Then cut out half of the smaller heart from the fold.

2.

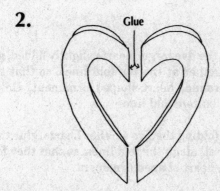

Glue

3.

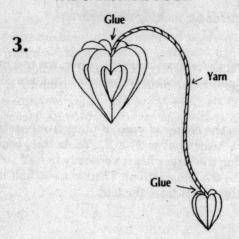

Glue

Yarn

Glue

3. Leaving the five larger hearts slightly folded, glue them together at the top fold lines, so that they form a round, heart-shaped ornament. Do not glue the bottom fold lines.

4. Slightly folding the five smaller hearts, glue them together all along the fold lines, so that they form a round, heart-shaped ornament.

5. Cut an 18" length of green yarn. Glue one end of the yarn to the center top (the cleft) of the larger heart-shaped ornament, and glue the opposite end of the yarn to the center top of the smaller heart-shaped ornament. Drape the yarn across a single tree bough so that one heart hangs above the other.

Cornucopias

Cornucopias, or horns of plenty, were extremely popular Christmas tree ornaments in Victorian England. They typically held small candies such as gumdrops, sugar plums, and peppermints. In your own cornucopias, you can continue the candy-holding tradition, or you can substitute flowers, tiny glass balls, potpourri, or anything else small enough to fit.

To make cornucopias, you need:

- Sheets of thin cardboard or heavy poster board
- Sheets of red and green construction paper
- Doilies or lace-paper trim
- Yarn to match or complement the construction paper
- Thin, spooled wire
- Glue (all-purpose)

Directions for making cornucopias:

1. Cut a piece of thin cardboard or heavy posterboard according to the pattern shown.

Cornucopias

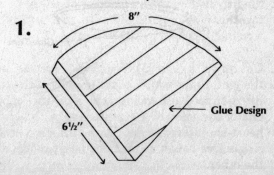

1.

8"

Glue Design

6½"

2.

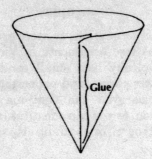

Glue

2. Cut construction paper to fit the cardboard piece, and glue the paper in place.

3. Shape the cardboard piece into a cone, with the construction paper side facing out. Glue all along the overlapped edges of the cardboard. Press the edges together firmly, and allow the glue to dry.

3.

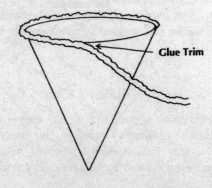

Glue Trim

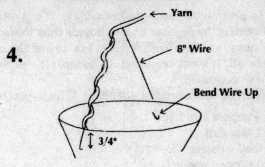

4.

← Yarn

8" Wire

Bend Wire Up

↕ 3/4"

4. Trim the circular lip of the cornucopia with doily sections or with lace-paper trim. Glue the trim in place.

5. To make the cornucopia's handle, first cut an 8" length of wire. Then poke one end of the wire ½" into the cornucopia, about ¾" below the lip. Bend the inside tip of the wire up to hold it in place. Next, poke the other end of the wire into a similar spot half way around the cornucopia, and bend the tip to hold it in place.

6. Wind yarn around the wire to cover it, making it stronger and more attractive. Leave enough yarn at either end to glue in place inside the cornucopia.

Baker's Clay

Conventional sugar, butter, or bread cookies are fragile and enticing. Therefore, they may not survive well as tree ornaments, depending upon the population being served by the tree. Try making cookie-style ornaments with baker's clay. It's a sturdy alternative to regular cookie dough that looks just the same; and although it doesn't taste just the same (after all, it's not meant to be eaten), it's perfectly safe if consumed.

For four to six ornaments about 4" high, you need:

- 4 cups white flour
- 1 cup salt
- food coloring*
- 1¼ cups water

Directions for making baker's clay:

1. In a large bowl, combine flour and salt. In a liquid measure, combine water and food coloring. Gradually pour water mixture and food coloring into flour mixture, kneading as you go along.

2. When clay is thoroughly kneaded and ready, use it to make ornaments, either by hand molding the clay or by rolling it out and applying cookie cutters. Completed ornaments should be able to lie relatively flat on a baking sheet.

3. When finished making ornaments, thread wire hangers through the top of each ornament.

4. Lay finished ornaments on a baking sheet, with hangers lying straight up (in proper hanging position). Bake at 275° F for 2½ hours. When finished, allow to cool for 15 minutes before handling.

Around 2 teaspoons of food coloring should provide a sufficiently rich color. Even better than food coloring is the same amount of powdered tempera paint, available at hardware and art supply stores. Be sure to get nontoxic paint. For most ornament-making sessions, two or three different colors of baker's clay are desirable.

CHAPTER 3

⚛ ⚛ ⚛

Decorations and Crafts

Whatever your year-round home decorating tastes may be, Christmas is a time when more is better. Use your imagination and the suggestions in this chapter to transform the place where you live into a scene of celebration.

Good Ways to Charm the Senses

1. Want to fill your home with a wonderful aroma? Toss cinnamon sticks, whole cloves, cut-up fruit skins (orange, lemon, apple, or banana), and bay leaves into a saucepan full of water. Bring the water to a boil, and then let the mixture simmer and steam.

2. To enhance the fragrance of a wood-burning fire, throw in pine incense, pieces of grapevine, or cedar chips.

3. For special holiday meals and festivities, carefully core green and red apples and use them as candleholders.

4. Buy separate spools of red, green, and gold velvet ribbon. Use lengths of these ribbons, in various combinations, as tie-backs for curtains and drapes, or as simple but elegant garlands and hangings.

5. Spell "Merry Christmas" with children's lettered blocks on a mantlepiece, table, or easily accessible piece of furniture. Let your family and guests try rearranging the letters to make different words.

6. Fill a large bowl or basket with solid-color Christmas tree balls, and set it where it can reflect light.

7. For an added touch of elegance, sprinkle a handful of gold glitter onto the center of a table set for dinner.

8. Buy small, Styrofoam tree forms from an art supply store. Then turn them into tabletop Christmas trees by covering them with gumdrops, nuts, mints, or tiny Christmas balls using a glue gun or pins (small children should always be supervised when working with pins).

9. For a creative alternative to a floral arrangment, buy a small sheath's worth of wheat from a florist, tie it with a fancy ribbon, and stand it upright.

10. Decorate your hearth with a festive Yule log. Wrap the log in a garland of greenery, or tie a wide ribbon into a bow around it, or adorn it liberally with sprigs of holly and mistletoe stuck into predrilled holes. You may even want to cradle the log in a basket of pinecones, wood chips, cotton, raffia, or straw. If you plan to burn the log, be sure to remove all ornaments first.

11. For a special nighttime effect, set several votive candles in glass holders in front of a window so that the light can be seen from outdoors as well as indoors. If you have double-hung windows, you can use the top ledge of the bottom window. Just be sure that the candle flames are not close to curtains or other flammable materials, and are not subject to drafts.

12. Drape strings of small lights (such as twinkle lights) around indoor doorways or the tops of walls.

13. Fill brandy snifters or clear glass vases with multicolored hard candies, and set them in easily accessible places.

14. Pyramids of fruits were very popular Christmas decorations during the eighteenth and nineteenth centuries. Make your own by mounting

apples, oranges, lemons, limes, and pineapples on wire or Styrofoam forms (avaliable at craft stores and art supply stores).

15. Strings of cranberries, or cranberries and popcorn, are not just decorative on trees. Try draping them around a room, or down a banister.

16. On party nights or Christmas Eve, line a walkway, driveway, patio, house front, fence, or curb with luminarias (candles anchored within large paper bags). Adapted from more ornate models popular in sixteenth-century Spain and Mexico, today's simpler luminarias are just as suitable for plain old fun as they are for sophisticated entertainment.

    To make a luminaria, fold the top of a grocery bag twice to form a secure cuff. Fill the bottom third of the bag with sand or gravel, and level the filling at the top. Then set a votive candle in a votive candle holder firmly into the center of the sand or gravel. Be sure never to leave luminarias unattended.

Tips for Decorating with Outdoor Lights

Only use light strings, bulbs, and extension cords that specifically state that they are designed for outdoor use, and be sure that they bear the "UL" (Underwriters Laboratories) insignia.

Avoid "octopus" connections and overloaded outlets.

The most attractive outdoor lighting schemes are consistent throughout. On the house itself, avoid mixing different styles of light strings (one solid-colored, another multicolored; or one blinking, another steady). You can decorate trees or shrubs in a different style than you decorate the house, but be consistent in all the tree or shrub decorations.

The handsomest lighting schemes on buildings are those that conform closely to selected architectural features such as window frames, doorways, and perimeter lines, rather than looping or crisscrossing.

Bulbs should not come in contact with flammable surfaces, bare metal, or the ground. It is best not to decorate with bulbs or wiring below the normal snow line in your area.

Make sure that no one can trip over outdoor wiring and cords.

Secure all lights and wiring well, in accordance with the instructions given. In trees and shrubs, be sure to allow some slack in the wiring so that high winds or heavy snows won't cause pull damage. For the same reason, avoid looping the wiring tightly around individual limbs.

If heavy snows encase the bulbs and wiring on trees and shrubs, avoid turning on the lights until you've knocked off the snow. When knocking off the snow, be especially careful not to damage the bulbs and wiring and not to inadvertently break frozen limbs.

Avoid leaving on outdoor lights when no one is home or when no one is awake at home.

Regularly inspect bulbs and wiring for safety. If individual bulbs are burned out, replace them as soon as possible.

Remove and store all outdoor lights immediately after seasonal use.

Card Tree

What are you going to do with the Christmas cards you receive? Many people like to hang them on a tree. Some choose the Christmas tree itself. Others prefer another, smaller tree reserved just for cards. Still others build a special tree for cards by securing leafless tree branches in a large pot filled with rocks. Here's a very practical and decorative alternative.

You need:

- A rectangle of gold or light green felt (sized according to the space to be filled and the estimated number of cards that will be received)
- A length of dark green felt (about the same amount of felt as the gold or light green rectangle)
- Two ¾"-thick dowel sticks, 2" longer than the width of the gold or light green rectangle
- Needle and dark green thread
- Scissors
- Piece of white chalk

Directions for making the card tree:

1. Using light, dotted lines, chalk a Christmas tree branch pattern onto the gold or light green felt, filling up most of the rectangle but leaving 2" borders at the top and the bottom. (Draw sample tree sketches on scrap paper first, to get the exact design you want.)

Card Tree

1.

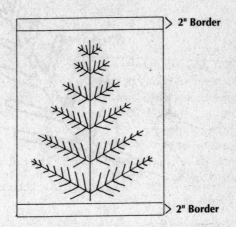

2" Border

2" Border

2.

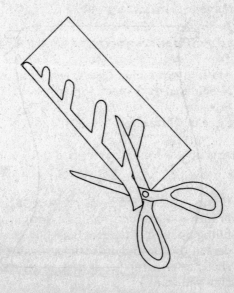

3.

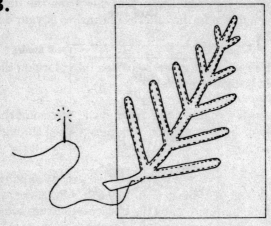

4.

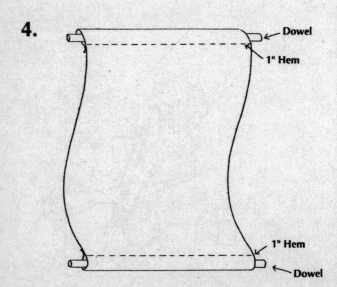

2. Cut out individual tree branches from the dark green felt to fit the different branches of your design.

3. Stitch the dark green branches into place on the gold or light green felt.

4. Make a 1" hem at the top and the bottom of the gold or light green felt. Slip a dowel rod through each hem.

5. Hang the card tree in the desired spot by slipping each end of the top dowel over a nail. As cards arrive, pin them onto the branches, letting some "greenery" show through between cards.

5.

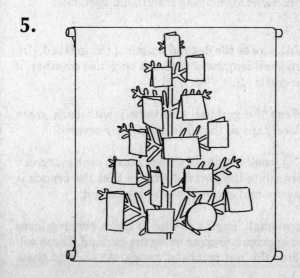

Traditional Garlands

One of the easiest and most effective Christmas decorations is a garland looped across the top of a wall or mantlepiece, around a window or doorway, down a banister or column, or wherever there's a continuous line that deserves good treatment. The materials mentioned below are widely available at nurseries and craft stores.

You need:

- Metal wire
- Wire cutters
- Dark green floral tape
- Artificial evergreen branches
- Eighteen-gauge floral wire

Directions for making traditional garlands:

1. Cut wire to the desired length of the garland. (Individual lengths of wire can be joined together, if necessary.)

2. Wrap the garland wire tightly with dark green floral tape so that it is completely covered.

3. Cut small lengths of wire to attach each evergreen branch to the garland wire so that the branch is secure and covers the wire beneath it.

4. Cut small lengths of wire to make hanging loops at appropriate spots along the garland. These will form the top points of swags. At each of these

spots, loop one of the small wires around the garland wire and twist it securely closed, leaving space to hang the loop over a tack or hook. If desired, decorate the garland with ribbons, bows, small ornaments, pinecones, or dried flowers.

Santa Boot Stocking

It used to be that children regularly wore long, thick, cotton stockings in the wintertime. These were perfect for holding lots of Christmas goodies. Nowadays, the traditional Christmas stocking, shaped like Santa's boot, serves as a worthy and beloved substitute.

To make your own stocking, you need:

- Two sheets of 12" × 15" paper (such as newspaper) and pencil
- Two pieces of red felt, 12" × 15"
- One piece of white felt, 12" × 15"
- Scissors
- Needle and thread (red and white)
- Absorbent cotton (preferably sheet-style)
- Fabric glue
- Small jingle bells
- Leather or braided fabric cord

Directions for making Santa boot stocking (see next page):

Christmas Stocking

1.

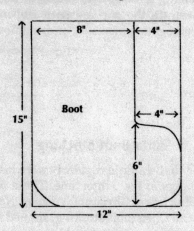

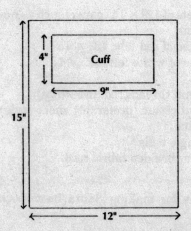

1. On one sheet of paper, draw an exact-size pattern for the boot, according to the model shown. On the other sheet of paper, draw an exact-size pattern for the cuff, according to the model shown. Cut out the patterns.

2. Pin the boot pattern to one piece of red felt and cut out the boot. Then reverse the pattern, pin it on the second piece of red felt, and cut out another boot. (The pattern is reversed on the second felt piece so that when the two halves of the boot are stitched together, each half will have the "good" side of the felt facing outward.)

2.

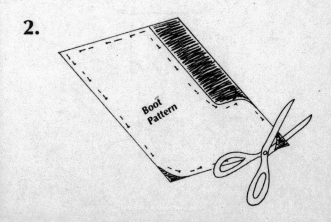

Boot Pattern

3. Pin the two boot halves together, so that the "bad" felt sides face inward. Then sew them together along the bottom and sides, using an overhand stitch. Leave the top of the boot open.

4. Pin the cuff pattern to the piece of white felt and cut out the cuff. Repeat for the other half of the cuff.

3.

4.

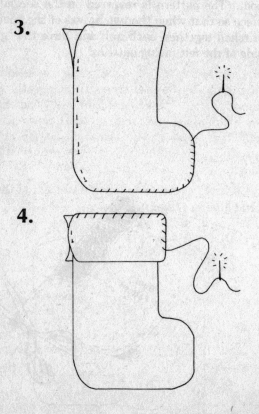

5.

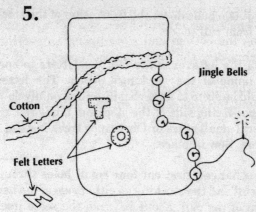

Jingle Bells

Cotton

Felt Letters

5. Center the two halves of the cuff across either side of the top of the boot (the cuff is slightly wider than the boot). Make sure that the "good" side of each half of the cuff faces outward. Sew each cuff half to the top of the boot using an overhand stitch. Then sew the two halves together at their sides with the same stitch.

6. Cut strips of cotton to line the bottom of the cuff and glue in place.

6.

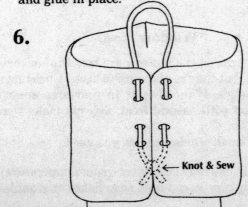

Knot & Sew

7. Sew jingle bells down the front seam of the stocking, from cuff to toe.

8. From the leftover white felt, cut letters to spell the name of the stocking's owner. The letters should be sized to fit vertically or diagonally down the out-facing side of the stocking. If desired, cut several small stars or Christmas trees instead of letters. Sew in place.

9. For a hanger, first cut four small holes through the cuff and the stocking on either side of the back seam of the cuff, about ½" from the seam itself. Thread one end of the cord through one set of holes, beginning from inside the stocking at the top. Thread the other end of the cord through the other set of holes in the same manner. Leaving a big enough cord loop outside the stocking to serve as a hanger, knot the two ends of the cord securely inside the stocking. Cut off any excess cord ends, and stitch the knot in place.

Window Frost

Frost patterns on the window are beautiful in their own right, but they're also sure to evoke Christmas-time nostalgia. If the climate in your area doesn't provide you with natural frost, why not make your own?

For six small window panes, you need:

- Slightly under ¼ cup water (room temperature)
- Slightly over ½ cup mild soap flakes or granules

- Medium-size bowl
- Several doily-style paper place mats
- Transparent tape
- Plastic foam sponge Directions for making window frost:

1. Pour water in the bowl. Add soap and beat (by hand or mixer) until the mixture is stiff enough to hold its shape.

2. Fit a place mat to a window pane. If the place mat is bigger than the window pane, cut the place mat to size, so that you can make maximum use of the doily edges. If the place mat is smaller than the window, cut the place mat in half, keeping intact the long top and bottom doily edges on separate halves.

1. **Window Frost**

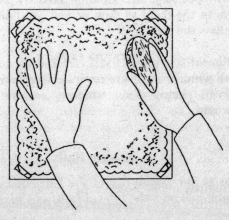

2.

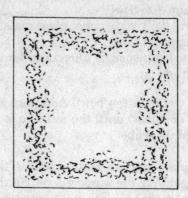

3. Temporarily tape the full or cut place mat to the window pane so that some or all of the edges of the window pane are covered, as much as possible, by the doily pattern.

4. Using the sponge, gently but firmly dab the whipped soap mixture over the doily pattern. Remove the doily as soon as you are finished, and allow the soap to dry.

5. Repeat this process, with fresh doily edges, until all window edges are covered. To remove window frost, simply clean windows as you normally would.

Kissing Ball

Prior to the popularity of the Christmas tree, the kissing ball was the typical focus of Christmastime celebration in English and American homes. In addition to kissing beneath it, Christmas celebrants hung presents from it or piled presents directly below it. This version is considerably smaller and more ornamental, ideal for a doorway or the center of a room.

To make the kissing ball, you need:

- Artificial mistletoe, holly leaves, and red berries
- Floral wire
- Wire cutters
- Dark green floral tape
- 7" embroidery hoop (two hoop pieces)
- 2 yards of ¼" red ribbon
- 2 yards of ¼" green ribbon
- Scissors

Directions for making the kissing ball:

1. Allowing approximately 8" or 9" to trail at each end, wind the red ribbon tightly around the smaller hoop piece. Tie the ribbon ends securely together where they meet on the hoop.

1.

Kissing Ball

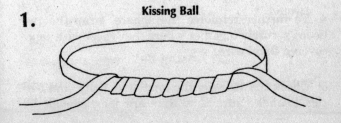

2.

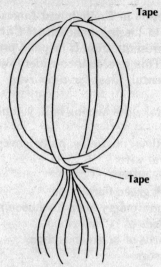

Tape

Tape

2. Using the green ribbon, follow the same procedure (step 1) on the larger hoop piece, leaving the tightening screw uncovered.

3. Place the smaller hoop piece inside the large one. Work the two pieces around so that they cross each other perpendicularly, forming a sphere, with the trailing ribbon ends of both hoops hanging directly downward. Tighten the screw so that the sphere holds shape.

4. To further reinforce the sphere, wrap the two hoops securely together where they meet with tape-covered floral wire.

5. Check the stems of the mistletoe, holly, and berries to make sure that they are long enough for

hooking onto the hoops where they meet at the bottom. If not, add more wire to the stems. Then wind floral tape tightly around the stems so that each stem is completely covered.

4. Hook the stem(s) of the mistletoe around the bottom of the ball so that the mistletoe hangs down from the ball, inside the trailing ribbons.

5. Hook most of the holly leaves and berries around the bottom of the ball so that some go inside and some go outside, framing the mistletoe without

3.

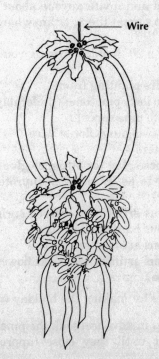

← Wire

obscuring it. Attach a few holly leaves and berries to the very top of the ball.

6. For a hanger, cut an appropriate length of wire (depending on where you want to hang it), wrap it tightly in floral tape, and hook it around the very top of the ball, where the hoop pieces intersect.

Holiday Wreath

The most popular spot for a wreath at Christmastime is hanging on the front door, where it can delight and and invite anyone about to enter. This wreath looks great there, or anywhere else you care to put it.

To make a 20" holiday wreath, you need:

- A 16" wire planting frame
- Thirty to forty pinecones (preferably long and narrow white pine cones)
- Twenty-two-gauge florist wire
- Wirecutters
- All-purpose glue (or stronger glue, if the wreath is going to be in an area unprotected from the weather)
- Numerous artificial evergreen sprigs
- Numerous hard-shelled nuts
- Numerous artifical red berries
- Numerous artifical edelweiss flowers (or artificial mistletoe)

Directions for making the holiday wreath:

1. Two days in advance, soak the pinecones in a tub of water until they close (approximately one

hour). Then insert the wet cones side by side into the frame, reversing the direction of every other cone. Allow a day or two for the cones to dry completely.

Holiday Wreath

1.

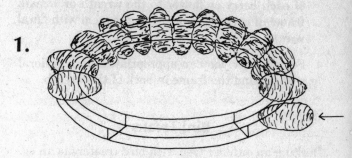

2. Laying the wreath on a flat surface covered by several thicknesses of newspapers, place the sprigs, nuts, berries, and flowers all around the wreath according to taste.

2.

3. When the sprigs, berries, and nuts are all arranged the way you want them to be, set about attaching them to the wreath. Glue the sprigs and nuts into place, holding each glued sprig or nut until the glue has begun to harden. Hook the stem of each berry or flower to the wreath or wreath frame (if necessary, lengthen the stem with floral wire).

4. For a holder, loop an appropriate length of floral wire around the frame in back of the wreath.

Bird Treater

Decking an outdoor tree with bird treaters is an excellent way not only to express your love for nature at Christmastime but also to add a festive look to your outdoor property—a look that remains attractive and appropriate well past Christmas itself.

To make a bird treater, you need:

- 4" aluminum foil pan
- Green, red, or gold paint
- ½" mesh hardware cloth, approximately 9" × 5"
- Metal wire
- Wire cutters
- Green, red, or gold yarn
- Suet mix (purchase ready-made at a nursery, or make your own following recipe on page 72)

Directions for making bird treater:

1. Roll the hardware cloth into a cylinder so that the diameter of the cylinder is only slightly smaller than the diameter of the bottom of the foil pan.

Bird Treater

1.

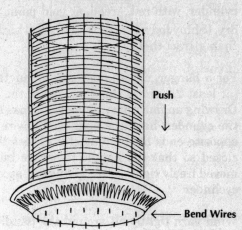

Push

Bend Wires

2. Centering the cylinder inside the pan, press down on the cylinder so that the ends of the wires poke through the bottom of the pan. Then bend these wires up to hold the cylinder firmly onto the pan.

2.

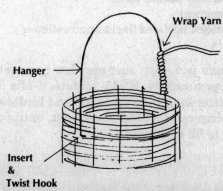

Wrap Yarn

Hanger

Insert
&
Twist Hook

3. Paint all exposed surfaces of the pan, outside the cylinder, with red, green, or gold paint. Allow to dry. (Shiny foil surfaces tend to repel birds, rather than attract them.)

4. For a hanger, cut an appropriate length of yarn (at least 2½ times the diameter of the cylinder. Drawing an imaginary diameter across the top of the cylinder, hook the ends of the wire into the opposite ends of the diameter. Twist the hooks closed so that the handle is secure but can be moved freely right or left, giving full access to the cyclinder.

5. Wind yarn tightly all around the handle so that it is completely covered. Tie securely at both ends of the handle.

6. Fill the cylinder with suet mix. If making your own, follow this recipe, which is sufficient for two to three fillings.

   1 pound ground suet
   ¼ cup crunchy peanut butter
   1 cup cornmeal
   2 cups mixed birdseed (including sunflower seeds)

In a medium pan, melt suet over low heat until liquid (approximately 10–15 minutes). Mix in peanut butter first, then cornmeal and birdseed. Cool in refrigerator, at least overnight, until you are ready to fill bird treater.

7. Immediately after filling, hang the bird treater on a tree branch that's visible from the house. If it's not possible or convenient to slip the hanger itself over a branch, use a piece of yarn to tie the top of the handle to the branch, making several loops with the yarn before tying.

8. Refill the bird treater as it is emptied by visiting birds. It may take several days to a couple of weeks for birds to discover your bird treater, so be patient.

CHAPTER 4

♠♠♠

Cards

Every year, year after year, Christmastime provides a unique opportunity to favor relatives, friends, and valued acquaintances with a special greeting, a card that serves as a tangible symbol of the sender's good wishes and best regards. Indeed, for many relationships, Christmas cards are a lifesaver. Timeless in sentiment and always appreciated, they are one of the most efficient means of sustaining or renewing relationships that otherwise might die of neglect.

No one knows how long greeting cards have been associated with Christmas. From all the historical evidence, commercially produced cards didn't appear until December 1843, when the English lithographer John Horsely printed 1,000 cards. Commercially printed cards were introduced into the United States in 1875 by Louis Prang, a German immigrant. Prang's ornate cards, adorned with ribbons, laces, and gilt, were instant successes and established the convention and fashion of Christmas cards for the next two decades.

At the turn of the century, the founding of the first mass-market card companies, including Hallmark (then Hall Brothers) and American Greetings, ushered in the era of modern Christmas cards. Compared to their showy, highly traditional predecessors, modern cards display a wide variety of styles and messages in a more streamlined, folded format.

However, commercially produced cards are only part of the story. During this same period of time, homemade Christmas cards also gained steadily in popularity. In fact, a 1991 Gallup poll found that 18 percent of Americans send homemade cards instead of manufactured cards—up 6 percent from a similar poll in 1981. A homemade card is a delightfully personal way to express one's thoughtfulness, as well as a wonderfully creative outlet, very much in keeping with the spirit of the season.

Manufactured or homemade, store-bought or specially ordered, a Christmas card helps both sender and receiver to capture the Christmas season in specific images. At the same time, it rekindles all the good memories that the sender and receiver share.

Cards for a Cause

Listed below are some representative organizations that sell holiday cards in order to benefit their particular cause. Orders can generally be filled within ten days. If you don't see your favorite charity, service, or advocacy group here, call it directly and inquire. Also ask about gifts, wrappings, and special donations.

Association for Retarded Citizens (ARC)
817-261-6003

Audubon Society
800-323-4359

The Children's Christmas Card Project
The M. D. Anderson Cancer Center at the University of Texas (Austin)
800-231-1580

End Childhood Hunger in America
Food Research and Action Center
800-934-4543

Gay Men's Health Crisis
New York City–based group offering support to persons with AIDS, regardless of sexual orientation
212-337-3519

The Humane Society
202-452-1100

Nature Conservancy
800-227-1114

Sierra Club
415-923-5500

UNICEF
212-686-5522

United Cerebral Palsy of Greater Birmingham (Alabama)
205-226-9105

World Wildlife Fund
800-833-1600

Ten Things to Do
with the Christmas Cards You Receive

1. Create a card tree (see "Card Tree," Chapter 3).

2. Hang each card on your Christmas tree or on a second, smaller tree reserved especially for cards.

3. In a hallway, or in the living room, dining room, or family room, tack lengths of string or strong thread in swags along the tops of the walls, just below the ceiling. Hang your cards by draping their spines along these lengths.

4. Arrange your cards in various stand-up groupings on the mantel, on side tables, and on the tops of large pieces of furniture. Or slip them under the glass of glass-topped tables or desks.

5. Tape your cards all over door surfaces that are usually in view.

6. Store your cards in a large, attractive basket or bowl placed near a chair, to encourage browsing.

7. After the season, cut out the covers or images of selected cards and use them on homemade cards for the next year.

8. After the season, cut out the covers or images of selected cards and glue them in scrapbooks for children, hospital patients, or nursing home clients to enjoy.

9. After the season, cut out the covers or images of selected cards and use them to make Christmas tree ornaments by gluing them to pieces of thin carboard or to three-dimensional forms.

10. After the season, cut out the covers or images of selected cards and use them to make a Christmas collage—a work of art that can represent that particular season in future years, when it can be used as a decorative hanging.

Potato Print Card

You can make a design printer out of many things besides a potato, including an apple sliced down one side, a carrot sliced across the width, a flat piece of Styrofoam, or a linoleum block. For card-making parties, you might try all of these options at once. However, the long-standing favorite printer of homemade card makers is a potato.

Before carving your design into the potato, according to the directions that follow, draw an exact-size model of the design on a piece of paper. The best designs are simple and clean-cut, and they are small enough so that they won't come closer than ½" to the edge of the potato. Bear in mind that the image you draw will be reversed in the final print. Adjust your drawing to suit your taste, as well as these requirements.

Once you have carved your design in the potato, try a few practice prints before actually making your cards. This practice session accomplishes two purposes. First, you can make sure that the print looks the way you want it to look: A little texture and roughness adds character to a design, but you don't want it to be indecipherable or ugly. Second, the printing surface will get thoroughly soaked, so that it will produce the strongest print it can.

In addition to or instead of the candy cane represented here, you might try a star, an angel, a Christmas tree, or three crowns (for the three kings).

For the potato print card, you need:

- One medium or large potato (preferably Idaho-style)
- Two knives: one large and one small
- Paint (preferably tempera)
- Paintbrush
- Paper for card (preferably heavy paper)
- Thin pad of old newspapers

Directions for making the potato print card:

1. Using a large knife, cut the potato in half so that you have a smooth, flat printing surface. If you cut cleanly, you will have two printers—the two halves of the potato—on which you can make different designs.

Potato Print Card

1.

Actual-Size Pattern

2. Blot dry the cut surface of the potato, and lightly paint the design onto it, using paint in the color you want to print.

2.

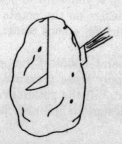
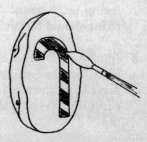

3.

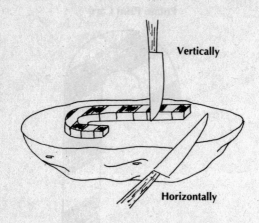

Vertically

Horizontally

3. Carve out the rest of the potato surface, outside the outline(s) of your design, so that your design will stand out in relief. To do this well, first use a small knife to cut into the potato about ¼" all the way around each outline. Then cut into the potato from the outer edge—horizontally and vertically—to remove individual blocks of potato.

4. Place folded card paper onto a thin pad of old newspapers, so that the side you want to print is facing up. Repaint the design on the potato (the paint should be fairly thick for a good print).

5. Immediately press the painted side of the potato onto the card paper. Apply some pressure, but don't bear down too hard. Lift the potato printer carefully. Repaint the design for the next printing.

4.

Stencil Card

A good stencil can provide you not only with stylish Christmas cards but also with attractive decorations like banners, posters, tablecloths, and gift wrap. Before you start, lay out newspaper or an old sheet to protect your work area. Then create the design you want—exact size—on a piece of scrap paper.

After you've made your stencil, according to the following directions, give it a few practice runs before actually making your cards. You may want to try out different ways of putting paint on your stencil design.

The best designs for a stencil consist of three or more cut-out shapes that are simple and not too small. Besides the Santa Claus suggested here, you might try a wreath, a Christmas tree, a holly leaf with berries, or reindeer hoofprints (virtually identical to deer hoofprints).

For the stencil card, you need:

- Stencil paper or thin cardboard
- Pencil
- Paint and paintbrush (preferably tempera)
- X-Acto knife or mat knife
- Construction paper for card

1.

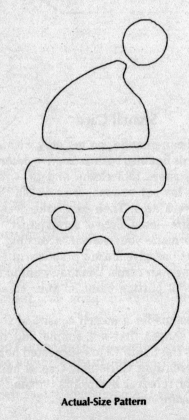

Actual-Size Pattern

Directions for making the stencil card:

1. Copy your design onto stencil paper or thin card-board. Make sure that the design is the right size for your card, and that you can leave at least 2" of space all the way around the design.

2. Carefully cut out the design shapes.

2.

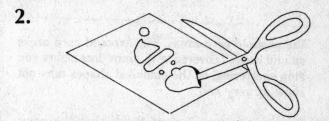

3. Lay the stencil over the front of the card and lightly tape the outside corners of the stencil in place. If necessary, cover all parts of the card except what shows through the stencil holes with scrap paper to protect it from paint splatters.

4. Lightly stroke or dab paint to cover all the card paper that shows through the stencil hole. Or you may want to spatter the paint onto the card instead of stroking or dabbing it.

   To spatter, first dab the bristles of an old tooth-brush or stiff paintbrush into the paint. Then hold the toothbrush with the bristles angled over the stencil holes and slowly run your finger over the bristles so that the paint lightly flickers across

3.

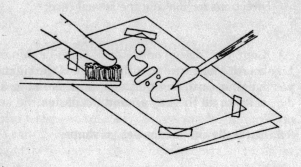

the exposed card areas. The exposed card areas should be well covered with paint dots before you stop spattering, or the stenciled shapes may not show up very well.

5. Remove the stencil carefully so that the paint doesn't smear. Allow the card to dry before adding your message and any details to the stenciled shapes. Also, check the underside of your stencil before reusing to make sure there is no wet paint there.

"Open Door" Photograph Card

Like an Advent calendar, an "open door" card invites you to pull back one image to find another image underneath—a motif that perfectly captures the surprise quality of Christmas. The card described below features a family photograph, mounted so that the recipient symbolically enters your home to meet you and your family. In place of the photograph, you can substitute any image that suggests a cozy, domestic Christmas scene.

For the "open door" photograph card, you need:

- Thin cardboard or poster board
- Scissors
- X-Acto or mat knife
- Family photograph (preferably with holiday trappings)
- All-purpose glue
- Sheet of construction paper (light colored, coordinated with photograph)
- Pencil and ruler
- Tempera paints (assorted colors for a doorway) and brush
- Brad-style paper clip (fold-back prongs)

Directions for making "open door" photograph card:

1. Using scissors, cut two rectangular pieces of cardboard so that they match exactly: one for the doorway, and one on which to mount the photograph.

   The precise dimensions of the cardboard pieces will depend on the size of your photograph. Each piece should be door-shaped; and it should allow for at least ½" of extra space along the top and sides of the photograph, and at least 1" of extra space along the bottom of the photograph.

2. Glue the photograph to one of the cardboard pieces, allowing for the extra space described above.

"Open Door" Photograph Card

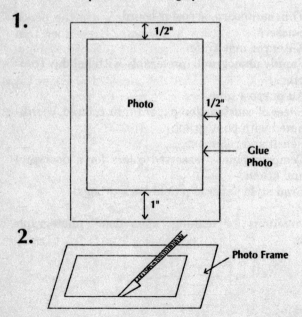

1.

1/2"

Photo

1/2"

Glue
Photo

1"

2.

Photo Frame

3.

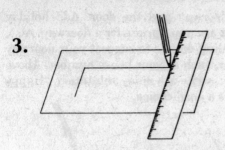

3. Using the X-Acto knife, cut out a frame for the picture from the construction paper: one that fits the full dimensions of the cardboard piece and slightly overlaps the edges of the photograph. Glue in place.

4. On the other piece of cardboard, use the pencil and ruler to draw a doorway. Remember that when this piece is mounted on top of the photograph piece, the door itself should open to reveal the photograph and a thin amount of frame (at least ½" of frame on the bottom).

4.

5. Paint the doorway and the door. Add holiday touches that are appropriate for a doorway. Also, consider adding details to suggest your doorway in particular, such as your house number. Above the doorway, write a holiday salutation: "Happy Holidays!" is a good choice.

5.

6. Using the X-Acto knife, cut the top, bottom, and right side of the door so that it can open. Fold it open carefully, so that there's a clean, straight fold along the left side.

6.

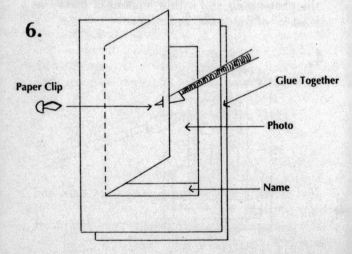

7. Apply glue to the back of the doorway piece (not to the door itself), and press that piece carefully onto the photograph piece, so that the photograph is properly framed within the open door space.

8. Write your name(s) below the photograph, on the construction paper frame.

9. Carefully stick the brad-style paper clip through the door so that it functions as a doorknob. To help ensure that the brad doesn't rip through the door, first make a slit for the clip with the X-Acto knife, not too close to the edge of the door.

3-D Tree Card

This card doubles as a three-dimensional decoration, making it a gift as well as a greeting. Before drawing and bedecking the poster board tree, sketch a same-size model on a sheet of scrap paper so that you know exactly what you want to achieve. Experiment with different ornament themes and styles to match the different recipients.

For the 3-D tree card, you need:

- Green poster board
- Pencil
- Scissors
- Assorted adhesive shapes such as stars, dots, and mini-stickers
- Metallic paints and paintbrush (available in art supply stores)

Directions for making 3-D tree card:

1. Carefully draw the outline of the tree on the poster board. To stand properly, the tree should have a broad, flat base (not a stem) that is approximately two-thirds the height of the tree.

3-D Tree Card

1.

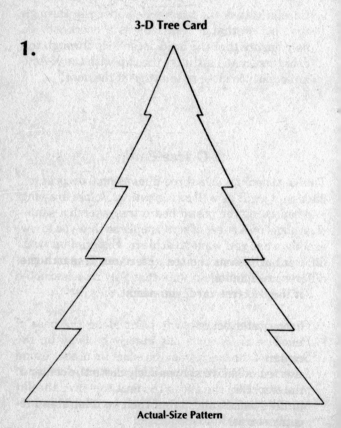

Actual-Size Pattern

2. Cut out the tree. Using this cut-out tree as a model, draw a second tree on the poster board.

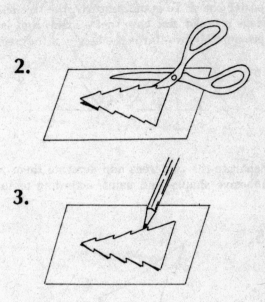

2.

3.

3. Cut out this second tree. Place one tree on top of the other and make sure that they match exactly. If they don't, trim them so that they do.

4. From the exact midway point along the base of the first tree, cut a slit exactly halfway up the center of the tree. From the exact tip of the second tree, cut a slit exactly halfway down the center of the tree. Slip the slit in the first tree over the slit in the second tree so that the two trees stand together on an X-shaped base.

4.

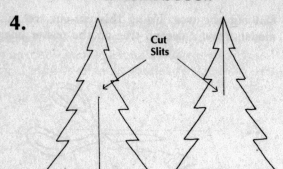

Cut
Slits

1   2

5. Separate the two trees and decorate them with adhesive shapes and paint, according to taste.

5.

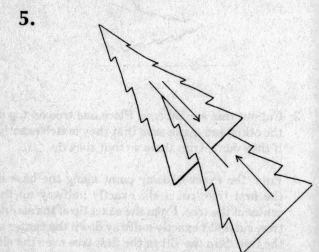

6. Bear in mind how the decorations on each single tree will look once the two trees are put together. Leave room to paint a message somewhere on the tree (perhaps as letters "dangling" from a garland)

6.

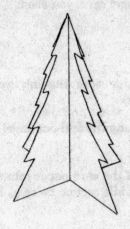

Fold-Out Angel Card

Behold, an angel card that spreads its wings to greet
the recipient! With its three inside panels for writing
(the two wings plus the middle), this card makes an
especially good party invitation.

For the fold-out angel card, you need:

- Card paper
- Pencil
- Scissors
- Colored pens (make sure the ink won't show
  through the paper)

Directions for making the fold-out angel card:

1. Fold the length of the card paper into three sections, with the middle section twice as big as the
   two side sections.

Fold-Out Angel Card

1.

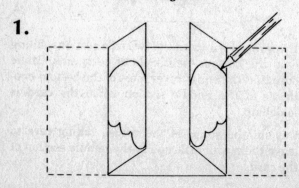

2.

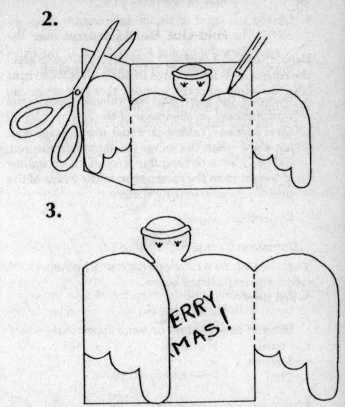

3.

2. Draw angel wings on the two side sections, filling only the bottom two-thirds of each side. Make sure that the wings cover most of the bottom two-thirds of the middle section when the card is folded up.

3. Cut out the shape of the wings, taking care to leave them well attached to the middle section of the card.

4. On the top third of the middle section, draw an angel's head so that the head pokes over the wings when the card is folded. Trim off the extra paper in the top third of the middle section.

5. Decorate the card with the colored pens. Write your message on the inside of the card, across all three sections, taking care that the message does not show when the wings are folded. (If desired, you can glue a rectangular piece of paper, lighter in weight than the card paper, to the inside of the card to use as a writing surface.)

Envelope

To make your own envelope for your Christmas card, follow the steps listed below.

You need:

- Sheet of paper (white or some appropriate color)
- Pencil
- Scissors
- Glue

Directions for making the envelope:

Envelope

1.

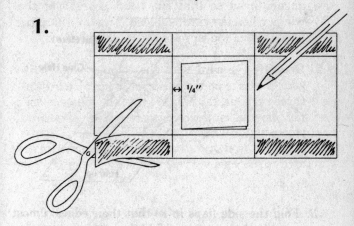

1. Cut a rectangle from the sheet of paper that is two times taller and three times wider than your card.

2. Place your card in the exact center of the paper and draw a rectangle around the card ¼" away from the outermost edges of the card. Set the card aside. Extend each line to the edge of the paper, and cut out the four corner rectangles. This will leave a cross-shaped piece of paper.

2.

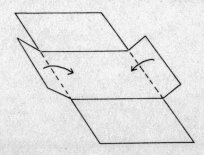

3.

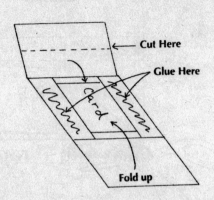

3. Fold the side flaps in so that their edges almost meet in the center, and fold the bottom up to cover the side pieces. Glue the side and bottom flaps together carefully.

4. Fold the top piece down, and draw a line across it 2" from the top. Cut off the rest of the top flap.

5. Put the card in the envelope and glue the flap shut, leaving the sides of the flap unglued. Send it to a relative or a friend.

CHAPTER 5

▲▲▲

Gifts and Wraps

The first recorded Christmas gifts were gold, frankincense, and myrrh, given to the Christ child by the the three wise men. After that, there is no record of any Christmas-related gift giving until the year 1200, when French nuns started bringing gifts to poor children's homes on the eve of December 6, Saint Nicholas's feast day, which was then considered the beginning of the Christmas season. Known for his many acts of charity, Saint Nicholas (or Saint 'Claus) ultimately evolved into Santa Claus, and gift giving ultimately evolved into a major element of celebrating Christmas.

The best way to choose a gift for someone is not to browse around in the stores until inspiration strikes. Before even going to the stores, you should think about that person carefully, summoning up images of how that person lives, what that person enjoys, and what that person might need. If no gift ideas come from this process, then review the suggestions offered in this chapter: They've been culled from lists of gifts with the broadest appeal in their demographic category.

Finally, give careful attention to the wrapping as well as the gift. The wrapping, too, can express your thoughtfulness and regard, and thereby move the opener to be very receptive to your gift, whatever it may be. The wrapping activities offered here are fun to do, and could form the basis of a great gift-wrapping party. Just make sure that party attendees are not wrapping gifts for each other, or there'll be no surprises under the tree.

Fifteen Gift Ideas for Children

1. Dollhouse furniture (good for play, whether or not the child has a dollhouse)
2. Costume kit for make-believing (box filled with crown, cape, wig, mask, glasses, etc.)
3. Rubber stamp with name plus ink pad or a seal with name plus wax
4. Hand puppet
5. Building blocks, cardboard bricks, or Lego blocks
6. Savings bank, partially filled
7. Modeling clay with pictures (cut out or drawn) of suggested creations
8. Assorted crayons, felt markers, pastel sticks, paints, and brushes for artwork, plus different kinds of paper or a draw-in scrapbook
9. Assorted balls in different sizes, colors, and styles

10. Trick objects from a magic store: dribble glass, plastic stain, ice cube with trapped bug
11. Bean bags
12. Purse, knapsack, pouch, tote bag filled with play objects and surprises
13. Book accompanied by a related toy and an audiotape of you reading the book
14. Oversized T-shirt with name, customized message, or colorful print
15. Mobile

Ten Gift Ideas for Teenagers

1. Compact disk (if you know recipient's musical tastes) or CD rack
2. Sports equipment (based on recipient's interests)
3. Tote bag (possibly filled with books or assorted practical and fun items)
4. Autographed photo of a celebrity the recipient likes
5. Geode bookends
6. Mirror in an unusual frame: wild and oversized, rustic and wooden, or fancy and artistic
7. Gift certificate or magazine subscription placed inside box of chocolates
8. Assorted novelty pins: photopins, message pins, and holograms
9. Knapsack
10. Oversized sweatshirt with logo of favorite group, cause, or team

Twenty Gift Ideas for Adults and Families

1. Picnic basket or kit
2. Board game
3. Photo album, already started
4. Pottery bowl
5. Candleholder(s) plus candle(s)
6. Hand-drawn, humorous map to recipient's home, plus numerous photocopies
7. Basket filled with high-quality food items such as exotic nuts, teas, spices, dressings, and home-made goods
8. Big glass jar or vase filled with candies or cookies
9. Humorous, puppet-style oven mitt
10. Assorted magnets for mounting notes and pictures on refrigerator
11. High-quality dish towels
12. Small, decorative pillow
13. Personally assembled bath kit with loofah
14. Heavy glass paperweight
15. Framed topographical map of recipient's area (check local map outlets for U.S. Geological Survey maps)
16. Personally assembled breakfast kit of teas, jams, syrups, pancake mix, pancake skillet
17. Special mug(s) filled with an assortment of useful and decorative items such as fancy pencil or pen, toothbrush, Christmas tree ornament, or kerchief
18. 1,000-piece jigsaw puzzle
19. Attractive and useful wooden box or tin filled with notecards and/or other small items

20. Plant in attractive pot, decked with tiny Christmas ornaments or garlands

Fourteen Gift Wrapping Ideas

1. Apply a stamp print or a homemade potato print to plain or solid-colored, porous paper, either before or after the gift is wrapped. (For instructions on making a potato print, see Chapter 4, "Potato Print Card.")

2. Paint a ready-made or homemade stencil design on plain or solid-colored, porous paper, either before or after the gift is wrapped. (For instructions on making a stencil design, see Chapter 4, "Stencil Card.")

3. Use acrylic paints, "tulip" paints, or paint pens (available in art supply stores) to create your own wrapping paper designs, perhaps including a personalized message. Metallic gold or silver paints or inks are especially attractive for this purpose.

4. Spray dried flowers with gold paint and tie them into the bow of the ribbon.

5. For a pleasingly natural look, use plain brown paper tied with raffia. Or instead of raffia, tie with twine and tuck in evergreen sprigs.

6. For a humorous touch, wrap presents in colored

comic sections of the newspaper, and tie them
with broad, red ribbon.

7. Instead of ribbon, use yarn, leather cords, or
   strips of fabric.

8. Instead of paper, use cloth: anything from satin,
   to cotton, to burlap, depending on your personal
   taste or the nature of the gift. If you're giving the
   gift to someone who likes to sew, consider wrapping it with a yard's worth of fabric that would
   make a nice trim, patch, or small craft. Tie your
   gift package with rickrack, a strip of lace, or
   yarn.

9. Wallpaper often works very well as wrapping paper, particularly if you need a strong paper to
   wrap a soft, flexible, or odd-shaped gift without
   a box. Use leftover footage or sheets from discon-
   tinued sample books (check with local vendors).

10. Save or purchase fancy paper shopping bags to
    use as gift bags. Tie the handles shut with a big
    bow that binds together lots of cascading ribbon
    streamers. (For making your own attractive,
    bag-style gift wraps, see "Spangled Bag" in this
    chapter.)

11. At a novelty store, purchase an assortment of
    tiny plastic animals, toys, and figures. Tuck or
    tie individual items into the ribbon when you
    wrap gifts. For certain gifts, you may want to
    choose a plastic item that's appropriate to the
    gift itself, to the recipient, or to yourself.

12. Create a special combo-gift by incorporating an item into the wrapping that not only relates to the gift inside, but also is useful in its own right. For example, instead of paper, you could use a dish towel to wrap a mug. Or you could tuck some pens under the bow of a package containing note cards. Or you could use shoestrings to tie a package containing a pair of shoes.

13. For a child's present, consider making an animal out of the wrapped gift. Use plain or solid-colored paper and add cut-out paper details, such as eyes, nose, whiskers, mouth, ears, legs, tail.

14. To create an elegant gift wrap for a round, soft, or odd-shaped gift, bag it in multiple layers of different colored crepe or tissue paper, each layer placed at an angle to the layer below it. Gather and tie the layers at the top with an attractive ribbon or cord, so that there's a fairly big topknot. Spread the topknot layers apart so that you see a portion of each paper layer.

Frosted Paper

Solid-colored wrapping paper that's been lightly spray-painted with white paint looks great under a Christmas tree. The frostlike effect is further enhanced if you spray-paint over a removable pattern to create an imprint in the "frost." Here a holly branch pattern is used, but you can use other patterns, as well as natural objects like ferns, leaves, or twigs (perhaps arranged in a Christmas tree pattern).

For frosted paper, you need:

- Card paper or light cardboard
- Scissors
- Solid-colored wrapping paper (preferably dark green)

Frosted Paper

1.

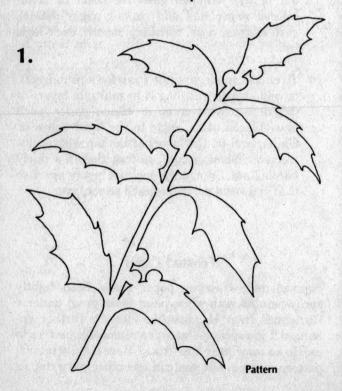

Pattern

- White spray paint (available at art supply stores)
- Dark green ribbon

Directions for making frosted paper:

1. From the card paper, cut out several copies of the the holly branch pattern shown.

2. Arrange the cutouts across the wrapping paper in the desired pattern.

3. Spray-paint lightly around the cutouts, keeping the can always in motion. Allow paint to dry before removing cutouts from paper.

2.

3.

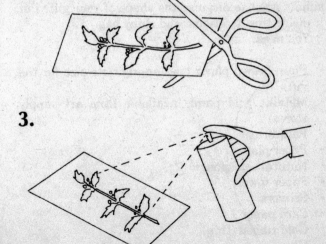

4.

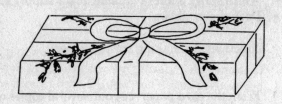

4. Wrap the paper around a gift and tie the package with dark green ribbon, making a relatively small, simple bow.

Spangled Bag

Do you have a gift that is hard to wrap? Or do you simply want to disguise the shape of your gift? Put it inside this handsome and shiny bag

You need:

- Plain brown paper bag (appropriate size for the gift)
- Metallic gold paint (available from art supply stores)
- Paintbrush
- Paper plate
- Natural sea sponge
- Paper towels
- Scissors
- Card paper
- Gold ribbon (thin)
- Glue

Directions for making spangled bag:

1. Lay the paper bag flat on a sheet of newspaper so that one side is facing up, with the bottom of the bag underneath. Then wet the sponge with water and wring it out.

2. Pour some of the paint into the paper plate. Dip in the sponge, and blot it on a paper towel.

Spangled Bag

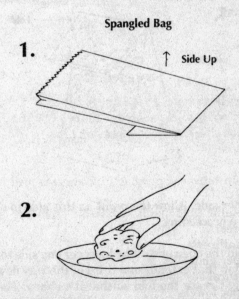

1.

↑ Side Up

2.

3. Repeatedly dab the sponge lightly across the surface of the bag, producing a randomly mottled surface that resembles a starry sky. Allow the paint to dry, then turn over the bag and dab-paint the

3.

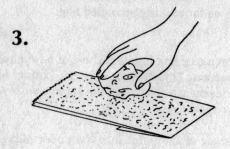

4.

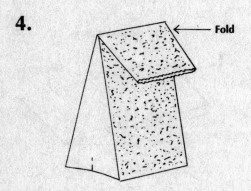

other side. Allow the paint on this side to dry before proceeding.

4. Fold the open end of the bag over one side to make a flap that extends one-third of the way down the bag. Crease the fold so that it's sharp. Then cut this flap so that it's rounded, like a half-moon.

5. Cut multiple lengths of gold ribbon, each long enough to extend from the bottom of the flap to the bottom of the bag.

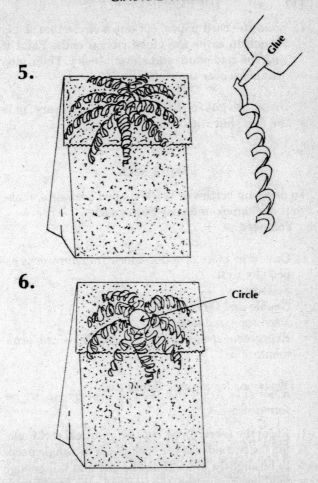

5.

Glue

6.

Circle

6. Curl each length of ribbon by running it lightly between your thumb and one blade of the scissors. Then glue the end of each ribbon to the center bottom of the flap, overlapping to create a central gathering point.

7. From the card paper, cut out a circle that is big enough to cover the glued ribbon ends. Paint it with the gold paint, and allow it to dry. Then, glue it in place over the ribbon ends.

8. Insert the gift in the bag, and, if necessary, glue the flap shut with a small dab of glue.

Santa Sack

To dress up bottles or brick-shaped packages, make your own quick-and-easy Santa sack.
   You need:

* One large piece of cotton fabric (muslin works especially well)
* Scissors
* Needle and thread
* Yarn rope (red or green)
* Evergreen sprigs (or other, similar-sized ornamentation)

Directions for making Santa sack:

1. From the fabric piece, cut two identical rectangles for the two sides of the sack. Each rectangle needs to be slightly wider than the gift and tall enough to allow for cinching the finished sack comfortably at the top (for bottles, cinching at the neck; for cylinders, boxes, or multiple items, cinching above).

Santa Sack

1.

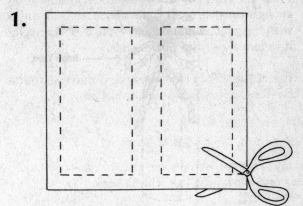

2. Place rectangles together, "wrong" surfaces facing outward. Sew together across bottom and two sides. Turn finished bag inside out so that "right" surfaces face outward.

2.

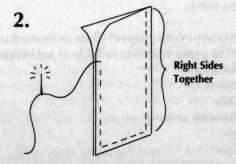

Right Sides Together

3.

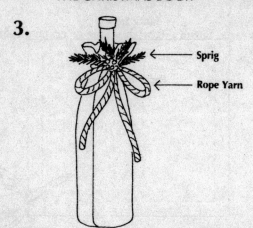

3. After filling with gift(s), cinch bag shut with yarn rope. Tuck evergreen sprigs behind the knot.

Paper Rose Wrap

Do what the Victorians did with their gift packages: Make old-fashioned paper roses to turn the act of gift wrapping, as well as the finished wrap, into something truly memorable.

You need:

- Tissue or crepe paper (white or desired color)
- Wide paper ribbon (available at art supply stores)
- Scissors
- Pencil
- Glue
- Tie wire or floral wire

Directions for making paper rose wrap:

1. Wrap a boxed gift with tissue or crepe paper.

Paper Rose Wrap

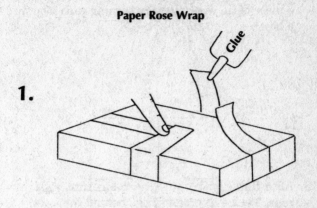

2. Cut two lengths of paper ribbon: one for each of the wraparound bars (allow for slight overlap with each piece). Wrap the lengths around the box so that all the ends meet in the center of the top of the box. Glue the ends of each piece in place, holding them down until the glue begins to harden.

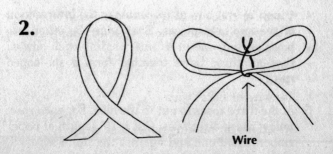

3. Cut three lengths of paper ribbon that are 1½ times wider than the box. With each ribbon length, make a loop and cinch it in the center with a piece of tie wire (thereby turning each loop into a bow).

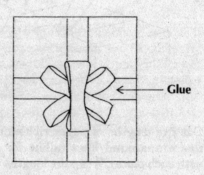

Glue

4. Glue the first bow at its center to the intersection of the two crosspieces. Then glue the other two bows on top, one at a time, angling each bow so that all three bows together form a six-looped nest.

5. Make three roses to put in the nest. For each rose, follow these directions: Cut a 15" length of paper ribbon. Hold one end against the tip of a pencil,

4.

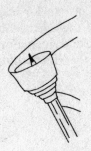

leaving a short piece of the end free for tying later.
Wrap the ribbon around the pencil, each layer on
top of the one below, as tightly as desired (the
looser the wind is, the more open the rose will be).
When the rose is the desired size, slide it carefully
off the pencil. Then, twist the ends of the ribbon
together, and bind the twist with tie wire. Cut off
any left-over ribbon.

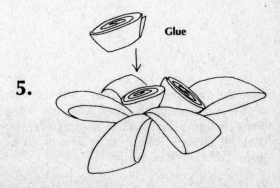

5.

6. Glue each rose into the nest of bows.

CHAPTER 6

♠♠♠

Activities and Events

Inevitably we find ourselves very busy during the Christmas season. The secret of enjoying the season and avoiding undue stress or depression is to make sure that we're busy the way we want to be. This chapter offers some great ideas for celebrating Christmas and other seasonal holidays with more pep and purpose.

Twelve Great Things to Do During the Christmas Season

1. If you live in a suburban or rural area where there's snow at Christmastime, check out places that offer sleigh rides. Arrange for your own

sleigh riding party, or join one already sched-
uled. In areas or times of no snow, you can often
find mock sleigh rides (on wheeled vehicles) or
hay rides.

2. Go on a holiday house tour. Often, historical
homes are specially decorated to reflect how
Christmas was celebrated during a particular
era in history. Check local periodicals for information.

3. Observe the four Sundays of Advent (the four
Sundays preceding Christmas) by maintaining
an Advent wreath. Make or buy a simple circle
of wire-linked evergreen boughs. Place four candles in holders just inside the wreath at equal
distance from each other, thereby forming a
square. Place a fifth candle in the center of the
square. Traditionally, the outer four candles in
an Advent wreath consist of three purple candles
and one pink candle, while the inner candle is
white (as an alternative, you can tie five white
candles with appropriately colored ribbons).

Every Sunday during Advent, have a small
ceremony in which you light a new candle (the
first Sunday, the first candle; the second Sunday, the first and second candles, and so on).
Save the pink candle for the last Sunday before
Christmas. Light the white candle on Christmas
Eve. The rest of the ceremony can consist of a
prayer, a special reading, a taking of turns to say
what was special about the week, and/or the
sharing of a holiday snack.

4. Instead of or in addition to an Advent wreath, keep an Advent calendar, available at most stores that sell cards. Especially compelling for children, Advent calendars feature a numbered flap for each day during the Advent season. On a given day, the flap for that day is folded back to reveal a unique image. Advent calenders are manufactured in religious and nonreligious formats (the nonreligious type feature images like Santa Claus, snowflakes, etc.).

5. Go caroling with a group: either a group organized by you, or a group soliciting participants. Check churches, community centers, schools, hospitals, retirement communities, and local periodicals. (Also see "Tips for Caroling," in this section.)

6. Arrange a time to go Christmas shopping with a friend. Include lunch and/or a movie.

7. Take in a musical concert or performance. In most areas, the Christmas season abounds with live, Christmas-related music: not only classical (sing-along Messiah concerts), but also pop, country, jazz, folk, reggae, or rock.

8. Go to a Christmas storytelling performance. Check local libraries and periodicals for listings.

9. Attend a parade. Many areas offer a variety of Christmas parades, some sponsored by businesses, others by schools, community groups, or institutions. Latinos often celebrate January 6,

the Twelfth Day of Christmas (also knowns as Epiphany or Three Kings Day), with a parade to represent the journey of the three wise men to Bethlehem.

10. Weather and climate permitting, indulge in some wintertime sport that you haven't tried for a while: ice-skating (which can also be done indoors), skiing, sledding, or ice hockey.

11. Weather and climate permitting, build a Christmas snow family: man, woman, child(ren), and pet(s). Remember that your snow sculptures stand a good chance of lasting longer if they are built in a fairly shady area and then gently sprayed or doused with cold water.

12. Instead of using an artificial Christmas tree or buying a cut tree from a street lot, make a special trip to a picturesque tree farm to cut your own tree. See Chapter 1, "Cut Trees," for guidelines.

Tips for Caroling

The following recommendations are made for so-called "traveling carolers," groups that sing as they walk around a neighborhood or that perform at one or more places, such as homes, hospitals, retirement centers, malls, schools, or businesses. Also, see Chapter 8 for lyrics to popular carols.

Everyone in the group should have his or her own

book or sheet containing lyrics for all the songs to be sung. Ideally, everyone should have the same book or sheet.

One person should be the leader, calling out songs to be sung, deciding when to begin and end singing sessions, and (if appropriate) acting as spokesperson. Determine in advance who the leader is, how all calls are to be made, how long performance sessions should be, and what the overall repertoire should be. It might be a good idea for the leader to carry a whistle for capturing the attention of all carolers at once, particularly when caroling or walking outdoors.

If possible, rehearse ahead of time, if only to determine the best songs and pitch for the group.

When standing in formation to sing, create several short, closely packed, semicircular rows of people, the taller people in the rear. This arrangement produces the most well blended sound.

Establish your itinerary ahead of time, notifying people for whom you wish to sing. If singing in a residential neighborhood, spread the word by mouth, note, or circular regarding when and where you'll be singing. It's nice to surprise people, but you can't surprise them when they're not even there to hear you.

If caroling or walking outside, follow these safety precautions:

- Check the weather ahead of time and plan accordingly (dress extra warmly, carry umbrellas or ponchos, go from place to place in cars, or reschedule).
- Closely supervise all young children that are caroling with the group. In any one group, the ratio of young children to adult should never be more than four to one.

- At night, wear light-colored outer garments and carry a lit flashlight. You do not have to carry the lit flashlight in your hand at all times: This would interfere with holding lyric sheets or books. Instead, it should be hooked to a coat or hung around the neck on a cord so that it's easily accessible by hand. It is just as important for the flashlight to illuminate you for motorists as it is for the flashlight to illuminate your path. .
- Whenever possible, walk on sidewalks instead of the road. If there are no sidewalks, walk facing the traffic. Cross streets at the corner, cooperating with any traffic lights or signs.
- Someone other than the leader should be appointed to carry a bag filled with extra scarves, gloves, mittens, stocking caps, and lyric sheets. Someone in the group or someone who joins the group in progress may need these items.

Avoid getting close to dogs and other pets while caroling. Even if certain animals are normally friendly to you, the strangeness of the circumstances might make them unusually aggressive.

Plan some wind-down activity right after caroling, such as a snack of hot cider and cookies.

Twelve Great Things to Do at a Home Party

Home Christmas parties generally take care of themselves: The place already looks festive with Christmas decorations, people are in a mood to enjoy themselves, and there's plenty of seasonal news to keep conversation rolling. Nevertheless, a little extra forethought and imagination can make your party a great deal more fun. Here are some suggestions.

1. Bust a pinata. The original Spanish and Mexican Christmas pinata was an animal-shaped earthenware shell filled with candies and trinkets. Celebrants hung it from a tree or a ceiling beam and took turns (often blindfolded) trying to bust it with a long wooden paddle. Today, in party goods stores, working pinatas—as opposed to strictly ornamental ones—tend to be made from papier mâché. Usually, you supply the contents, stick, and, if desired, the blindfold.

2. If it's a family party, look at old photographs together, swap stories, and reminiscence about family history.

3. Turn your Christmas party into a costume party. Specify a Christmas theme. Costume possibilities include an elf, a snowperson, Santa, a drummer boy, a shepherd, an angel, Scrooge, or a Christmas tree (either dressed as a tree, or just wearing ornaments).

4. Have Santa appear at your party to distribute small gifts (perhaps gag gifts).

5. Have a cookie-decorating party. Provide (or have people bring) plain, flat cookies; bowls of different icings; various confections such as sprinkles,

cinnamon dots, and M&M's that can be used as cookie decorations; knives and other utensils for decorating cookies; dropcloths for protecting cookie-decorating surfaces; and boxes or bags for taking decorated cookies home afterward. For homemade cookie suggestions, see Chapter 7.

6. Have a grab-bag at your Christmas party. Each guest brings an inexpensive gift (perhaps a gag gift) to put in the bag. Once the bag is filled, guests take turns drawing a gift from the bag. If desired, you can specify a theme for the gifts, such as "something to wish on" or "something to start the New Year with". Be sure to have extra gifts on hand for those people who might forget to bring one.

7. Have guests sign a Christmas guest book or, with a fat-tipped felt marker, a big panel of poster board mounted on the wall. In addition to their name, have them add messages. You might suggest that they mention a particular way that they'll be celebrating Christmas this year, or what they're looking forward to in the coming year, or a fantasy gift they'd love to receive.

8. Have a tree-decorating party, asking each person to bring one ornament (you supply the rest of the stuff). The tree being decorated could be your one-and-only Christmas tree, or, better yet, it could be a second, simpler tree that features only decorations brought and/or hung by guests during the season.

9. Create tags identifying different, fairly well-known people or images associated with the holiday season (Rudolph the Red-Nosed Reindeer, the Rockefeller Center Christmas tree, Jimmy Stewart [from *It's a Wonderful Life*], and chestnuts roasting on an open fire). As each guest arrives, attach a tag to his or her back. Tell the guest not to look at that tag, but to establish what it says by asking help from the other guests (any question but a direct, "Who or what am I?"). This game is an especially effective icebreaker if many of the people at the party don't know each other well.

10. Weather, climate, and laws permitting, have a bonfire, not only to evoke memories of Christmastime hearth fires, but also to symbolize the winter solstice season, when light returns to the earth as the hours of daily sunlight begin increasing.

11. Stage a fun, informal variety show, signing up guests in advance to perform various acts. Leave it up to individual guests to decide what acts they want to do, but be prepared to provide suggestions.

12. Follow the time-honored Christmas party tradition and sing Christmas carols. If you don't have anyone to play the piano, consider hiring someone; and be sure to provide lyric sheets. See Chapter 8 for lyrics to popular carols.

Twelve Ways to Be Kind
During Christmas

1. Buy or make a number of small gifts, wrap them,
   and put them in a big, decorated basket or box
   near your front door. Give them out to friends
   who come to call or to people who regularly make
   deliveries at your door.

2. Leave a small gift in your mailbox for the person
   who delivers your mail.

3. Clean out your closets, and take any clothing
   that you can spare to a nearby shelter for the
   homeless.

4. Call local churches, synagogues, community centers, and community service organizations and
   see if they have any tasks that you can volunteer
   to perform.

5. Organize a caroling group for entertaining your
   neighborhood, a hospital, or a retirement center
   (see "Tips for Caroling" in this chapter).

6. Offer to arrange a party for your kids, encour-
   aging them to invite school friends and, if desired, their schoolfriends' parents.

7. Make special long-distance calls to friends with
   whom you haven't spoken in a long time.

8. Tell a heartwarming story to a child, a group of children, or a mixed child-and-adult group. See Chapter 8 for recommended stories and story collections.

9. Contact friends or relatives who are elderly, sick, or under a great deal of pressure and volunteer your help for shopping or household chores.

10. Do something spontaneous and thoughtful for a neighbor: Shovel the driveway or leave a simple but attractive surprise Christmas present (such as an ornament or plate of cookies) on the doorstep.

11. Make Christmas resolutions to resolve old feuds, to straighten out misunderstandings, and to make new friends.

12. Take every opportunity to toast the good qualities and achievements of friends and family members.

Other Seasonal Holidays and Celebrations

Besides Christmas Eve and Christmas Day, there are numerous other holidays and celebrations around the time of the winter solstice (December 20–21):

The Twelve Days of Christmas

Traditionally, the twelve days of Christmas, beginning on Christmas Day and extending through January 6, commemorate the journey of the three wise men to pay homage to the Christ child in Bethlehem. Historically, however, the twelve-day Christmas celebration evolved as a Christian adaptation of the ancient Roman festival of Saturnalia, a very popular, twelve-day holiday celebrating Saturn, the father of all the gods.

In addition to Twelfth Day, or Twelfth Night, January 6 is also known as Three Kings Day (as well as Epiphany, the day of Christ's baptism). It is customary to bake a cake to be eaten on this day that contains one or more symbolic tokens. The most common token is a bean, to represent the king or queen of the day (whoever finds the bean in his or her piece becomes the monarch). Other possible tokens include a coin (wealth), a pea (wisdom), a thimble (patience), a heart-shaped item (devotion), or a clove (laughter, and status as jester of the day). If you plan to follow this token-in-a-cake custom, take care not to bake things into your cake that might go undetected until swallowed, or that could cause problems if they were swallowed or bitten!

To complicate matters, January 6 is also Christmas Day in the Eastern Orthodox Church, which did not move Christmas to comply with the twelve-day Julian calendar reform introduced in the eighteenth century. At any rate, January 6 is generally accepted as the last day to display Christmas decorations.

Hanukkah (or Chanukah)

Jews celebrate Hanukkah for eight days near the

winter solstice. Precise dates in the Julian calendar vary from year to year, as the date is calculated in the Hebrew calendar from the twenty-fifth day of the month of Kislev to the second day of the month of Tebet.

Also called the Feast of Lights or the Feast of Dedication (in Hebrew, *hanukkah* means "a dedicating"), Hanukkah commemorates the victory of a small band of Jewish warriors over the superior forces of a Syrian army that beseiged Jerusalem in 165 B.C. After their victory, the Jews purified the Temple of Jerusalem in an eight-day ceremony of mirth and gladness. The ceremony featured a miracle: Although Judah Maccabee, the leader of the warriors, could find only one day's supply of oil for the temple lamps, that supply lasted the full eight days.

Today, annual Hanukkah celebrations feature lighting a candle of the menorah, an eight-candle lamp, for each day of the festival (sometimes eight separate candles are used in place of a menorah). It is also customary to feast and exchange gifts. Among the traditional foods associated with Hanukkah feasts are potato latkes (crisp pancakes), kugel (a cake made with fruits, nuts, and matzo), and roasted, stuffed chicken.

Kwanzaa

Founded in 1966 by Mulana Karenga, head of black studies at California State University at Long Beach, Kwanzaa (from the Swahili *matunda ya kwanza*, meaning "first fruits") is a seven-day African-American festival that runs from December 26 through January 1. It celebrates African-American culture and community with feasting, storytelling, and symbolic activities; and, because of its strong appeal to families and social networks, that are already predisposed to draw closer together at this time of year, it is rapidly gaining popularity throughout the United States, Canada, and the Caribbean.

Each day of Kwanzaa is dedicated to one of seven principles illustrated by African proverbs:

1. *Umoja* (unity)
2. *Kujichangulia* (self-determination)
3. *Ujima* (collective work and responsibility)
4. *Ujamaa* (cooperative economics)
5. *Nia* (purpose)
6. *Kuumba* (creativity)
7. *Imani* (faith)

Each family or group celebrating Kwanzaa determines on its own how to express these principles in ceremonies and activities.

Yule

Yule is a festival honoring the winter solstice (December 20–21) that originated in pre-Christian North Europe. The word "Yule" derives from "Yolnir," a Norse name for the Teutonic light-bearing god, Odin. The primary focus of ancient Yule celebrations was feasting well into the night while burning a large, long-lasting log in Odin's honor to symbolize the return of light to the world.

Today, neopagans as well as many Christians continue the custom of burning a Yule log to celebrate new light in the world. They also follow other Yule customs such as hanging mistletoe in doorways for love and protection, bringing an evergreen tree into the house to symbolize the ever-renewing cycle of life, and making toasts with wassail. More traditional ways to celebrate Yule include having a bonfire, staging mock battles between darkness and light (with light always winning, of course), telling stories (especially heroic ones of overcoming death), and circle dancing.

CHAPTER 7

♠♠♠

Food and Drink

Eat, drink, and be merry with the suggestions in this chapter. And don't forget that Christmas treats make good gifts, too.

Cookie Decorating

Whether you're making and decorating cookies all by yourself or throwing a cookie-decorating party, you need to plan ahead carefully so that all the requisite materials are ready when you are. Use the cookie recipe and guidelines in this section, and follow this timetable:

1. Bake several batches of the Classic Christmas Cookie (no more than three days in advance).

2. Make piping cones (as many as you think you need: at least one cone for every icing color).

3. Clear table space for decorating. If needed, lay down a plastic sheet to protect the table surface.

4. Gather together cookie cutters, table knives (for spreading icing on the cookies), plates filled with add-ons, and trays or containers to hold decorated cookies.

5. Make Classic Christmas Icing in several colors, and put in separate bowls.

Classic Christmas Cookies

(Makes 5 to 6 dozen cookies)

To make Classic Christmas Cookies, you need:

1	cup butter or margarine, softened
1	cup sugar
2	eggs
1	teaspoon almond extract
3	cups all-purpose flour
1½	teaspoons baking powder
½	teaspoon salt

Directions for making Classic Christmas Cookies:

In large bowl, whip butter until smooth. Gradually add sugar, eggs, and almond extract. In another bowl, combine flour, baking powder, and salt. Gradually add to butter mixture, whipping constantly until well blended. Remove dough from bowl, and knead by hand to remove clumps. Divide dough into two circular mounds. Wrap and chill mounds in refrigerator until firm (at least 30 minutes; may remain in refrigerator up to 1 week). Preheat oven to 350° F. Remove one mound of dough from refrigerator, and place on lightly floured surface. Roll out dough into a rough circle about 1/4". Using cookie cutters or a wet table knife, cut out desired shapes from the dough. When all shapes are cut, gently separate unused dough and pat into a ball for later rerolling. Using a spatula, place cut-out cookies onto lightly greased baking sheets, and bake in oven for 10–12 minutes, or until light brown. Remove cookies from sheet and allow to cool for at least 10 minutes before decorating.

Piping Cones

To make piping cones for producing thin streams of icing, take a plastic bag (the commercially produced, freezer-storage kind) and snip off one corner. Funnel the icing through the top and squeeze icing through the hole. Start with a very small snip and enlarge gradually if necessary. For better results, attach an icing tip to the hole.

Add-Ons

Add-ons are ingredients that you apply to your Classic Christmas Cookies to add color, texture, taste, or specific details. Among the add-ons you might consider using are:

- Shredded coconut (comes in white and various colors)
- Sugar sprinkles (assorted flavors and shapes)
- Cinammon dots ("redhots")
- M&M's
- Silver dots (a hard confection resembling a tiny ball bearing)
- Miniature chocolate or butterscotch drops, including nonpareils
- Confectioners' sugar
- Chopped nuts (almonds, walnuts, or peanuts)
- Gumdrops, leaves, or slices (cut up or whole)
- Candied fruits (cut up or whole)
- Raisins

Classic Christmas Icing

(Makes about 3 cups)

To make icing, you need:

1   16-ounce package confectioners' sugar,
    divided
3   egg whites
½   teaspoon cream of tartar
½   teaspoon lemon juice, strained
    Food coloring (various colors)

Directions for making icing:

In large bowl, combine half the sugar and all other
ingredients except food coloring, and beat until
well blended. Add remaining sugar, and beat until
thick. Divide frosting into bowls, and color each
bowlful as desired, adding only 3–4 drops at a
time.

Gingerbread People
(Makes 8–10 people)

The spicy, nostalgic taste of gingerbread makes it perfect for a Christmas treat. Bear in mind that gingerbread cookies also make excellent Christmas decorations, on or off the tree.

To make Gingerbread People, you need:

½	cup butter
½	cup brown sugar
½	cup molasses
1½	teaspoons white vinegar
½	teaspoon vanilla extract
1	egg
3	cups all-purpose flour
¾	teaspoon ground ginger
½	teaspoon baking soda
½	teaspoon ground cloves
½	teaspoon ground cinnamon
¼	teaspoon salt

Directions for making Gingerbread People:

In large bowl, whip butter, sugar, molasses, vinegar, vanilla extract and egg until well blended. Combine all dry ingredients. Gradually whip into butter mixture until well blended (if possible, use mixer at low speed). Remove dough from bowl, and knead by hand to remove lumps. Cover and chill in refrigerator for at least 30 minutes. Preheat oven to 350° F. Remove dough from refrigerator, and place on lightly floured surface. Roll out in rough circle about 1/4" thick. Cut out gingerbread people with cutter or wet table knife. Separate unused dough and pat into a ball for later rerolling. Using a spatula, gently lift cut-out cookies onto a lightly greased baking sheet. Bake for approximately 10–12 minutes, or until golden brown. Remove from sheet and allow to cool for at least 10 minutes before decorating.

Shortbread Cookies

(Makes 60–70 cookies)

Cookies made of shortbread are popular all year long in the United States, but they are traditional Christmas treats in many parts of Europe. This recipe is a variation of the Greek Christmas cookie called *kourabiedes*. You need:

4	sticks butter
¾	cup confectioners' sugar
1	egg, beaten
1	teaspoon vanilla extract
4½	cups all-purpose flour
2	teaspoons baking powder
2	cups chopped walnuts

Directions for making Shortbread Cookies:

Preheat oven to 350° F. In large bowl, whip butter until it is smooth. Gradually mix in sugar, egg, and vanilla extact. Combine flour and baking powder in a separate bowl. Gradually whip into butter mixture until well blended. Spread chopped walnuts across lightly floured surface. Remove dough from bowl, and knead with hand to remove lumps. With floured hands, mold pieces of dough into walnut-size balls. Roll each ball across the chopped walnuts, so that the ball's surface is randomly studded with walnut pieces. Arrange cookies on lightly greased baking sheet. Bake for 12–15 minutes, or until a light tan color (not brown). Remove from oven, and allow to cool at least 10 minutes. Sprinkle with confectioners' sugar.

Almond Lace Cookies

(Makes about 50 cookies)

Lace cookies have been Christmas favorites in Europe and the United States since Victorian times. For Almond Lace Cookies, you need:

⅓   cup corn syrup
⅓   cup butter
½   cup sugar
¼   teaspoon almond extract
½   cup all-purpose flour
½   cup blanched almonds, finely chopped

Directions for making Almond Lace Cookies:

Preheat oven to 375° F. In medium saucepan, heat corn syrup until it boils. Reduce heat, and add butter and sugar. Cook until mixture is gold and foamy. Remove mixture from heat. Gradually stir in all other ingredients. On lightly greased baking sheets, drop teaspoonfuls of batter about 3" apart. Bake about 6 minutes (or until light brown with bubbling centers). Allow to cool for 30 seconds on baking sheet. Then remove gently and cool on wire rack at least 10 minutes. If cookies cool too long on the baking sheet, they may stick. In that case, return sheet to the oven for 30 seconds to unstick.

Christmas Cartwheels

(Makes 70–80 cookies)

These cookies are fun to make, attractive to look at, and delicious to eat. You need:

Dough

½	cup butter
1	tablespoon milk
1½	teaspoons vanilla extract
1	egg
2	cups all-purpose flour
1	cup sugar
½	teaspoon baking soda
½	teaspoon baking powder
¼	teaspoon salt

FILLING

2	tablespoons butter, divided
½	cup sugar, divided
2	teaspoons allspice, divided
2	teaspoons cinnamon, divided
1	cup walnuts, finely chopped, divided
1	cup dates, finely chopped, divided

Directions for making Christmas Cartwheels:

For dough, in large bowl, mix butter, milk, vanilla extract, and egg until well blended. In a separate bowl, combine flour, sugar, baking soda, baking powder, and salt. Gradually blend into butter mixture. Divide dough into two sections. Cover each section separately, and refrigerate until firm (at least one hour). Remove one section of dough from refrigerator. On lightly floured surface, roll out to 9" × 12" rectangle (make sides as straight as you can). For filling, melt 1 tablespoon butter, and brush across top of rectangle. Combine 1/4 cup sugar, 1 teaspoon allspice, and 1 teaspoon cinnamon, and sprinkle across top. Sprinkle 1/2 cup walnuts and 1/2 cup dates across top, and gently press into dough. Starting with a 12" side, jellyroll dough tightly. Wrap in plastic wrap and refrigerate until firm (at least one hour). Repeat filling process with second section of dough and the other half of filling ingredients. Preheat oven to 350° F. Remove two dough rolls from refrigerator. Cut each roll crosswise into 1/4" slices. Place slices 1/2" apart on lightly greased baking sheets, and bake for 10 minutes (or until golden brown). Remove cookies from baking sheet, and allow to cool at least 10 minutes.

Pfeffernuesse

(Makes about 100 cookies)

The word *Pfefferneusse* is German for "pepper nuts," but these tiny, ball-shaped Christmas treats are equally beloved in Sweden (as *pepparanoter*) and Denmark (as *pepernoder*). Right out of the oven, they're nutty-hard; therefore, the ideal arrangement is to make them a couple of weeks before eating, and keep them stored in an airtight container to soften. They're well worth the wait.

To make Pfeffernuesse, you need:

3	eggs
1	cup firmly packed light brown sugar
3	cups all-purpose flour
¼	teaspoon baking powder
	a pinch of salt
¼	teaspoon black pepper
1	teaspoon ground cinnamon
½	teaspoon ground cloves
½	teaspoon nutmeg
½	teaspoon allspice
1½	teaspoons grated lemon zest (colored part of peel)
½	cup blanched almonds, finely chopped
½	cup confectioners' sugar

Directions for making Pfeffernuesse:

In large bowl, beat eggs until fluffy. Gradually stir in brown sugar, flour, baking powder, salt, and spices until well blended. Stir in lemon zest and almonds: Wrap dough in plastic wrap, and refrigerate until firm (about one hour). Preheat oven to 350° F. Remove and uncover dough. Prepare lightly greased baking sheets. Roll tablespoonfuls of dough into balls, and place on baking sheets, 1" apart. Bake 15 minutes, or until light brown. Remove from sheets, and allow to cool for at least 10 minutes. Pour confectioners' sugar in a bag. Put cooled cookies into bag and shake until coated.

Yuletide Rum Cake

(Makes 10–12 servings)

Nothing tops off a hearty, Christmastime dinner better than a good rum cake. To make Yuletide Rum Cake, you need:

Cake

1	cup butter
1¼	cups sugar
2	cups dates, finely chopped
2	cups walnuts, finely chopped
1	cup golden raisins
1	teaspoon vanilla extract
1	teaspoon baking soda
1	cup water, boiling
3	eggs
2¼	cups all-purpose flour
1	teaspoon salt
1	teaspoon cinnamon
3	tablespoons rum
1	teaspoon salt
1	teaspoon cinnamon
3	tablespoons rum

Hard Sauce

1   stick butter
¾   cup confectioners' sugar
2   tablespoons sugar (granulated)
1   egg white, beaten
2   tablespoons rum

Directions for making Yuletide Rum Cake:

Preheat oven to 300° F, and lightly grease 9" × 13" × 2" baking pan. In large bowl, mix butter and sugar until well blended. Add dates, nuts, raisins, and vanilla extract. Combine baking soda and water, and pour into butter mixture. Add eggs and blend. In another bowl, combine flour, salt, and cinnamon, and gradually stir into butter mixture until well blended. Add rum and stir. Pour batter into baking pan, and bake for 1½ hours, or until firm in the center (a toothpick stuck into center comes out clean). Cool in pan for 1 minute. Remove from pan, and allow to cool at least 10 minutes on wire rack. Meanwhile, make Hard Sauce to serve with cake.

To make Hard Sauce, in a small bowl, combine butter, confectioner's sugar, and granulated sugar, and mix until fluffy. Add beaten egg white, and blend. Beat in rum. Place in serving dish to serve with cake.

English Wassail (or Mulled Cider)

(Makes 16–20 servings)

In England, wassail has long been the drink of choice on all twelve days of Christmas. During the Middle Ages, poor people used to go door to door at Christmastime caroling for wassail. Toast was served with wassail for dunking, and the recipient's first drink-and-dunk was customarily accompanied by good wishes for the donor, which is widely considered to be the origin of the expression "drinking a toast."

To make English Wassail (or Mulled Cider) you need:

1 gallon ale or dark beer (if a nonalcoholic beverage is desired, substitute 1 gallon apple cider, which makes this Mulled Cider instead of English Wassail)

1 cup brandy (optional)

2 cups brown sugar (omit if using apple cider instead of ale)

2 teaspoons grated lemon zest (the colored part of peel)

2 teaspoons grated orange zest

1 teaspoon ground ginger

1 teaspoon ground cloves

1 teaspoon ground nutmeg

1 teaspoon ground cinnamon
  Cinnamon sticks (optional)

Directions for making English Wassail (or Mulled Cider):

In large pan or pot, heat the beer and brandy (for English Wassail) or cider (for Mulled Cider). Avoid boiling. When beer mixture (or cider) is warm, add brown sugar (if using beer and brandy), lemon zest, orange zest, and ground spices over very low heat. Gently stir until all sugar is dissolved. Pour into punch bowl or cups for serving. If in cups, garnish with cinnamon sticks.

CHAPTER 8

♠♠♠

Stories and Carols

Christmas is a season of wondrous tales, some told in prose, others in song. May the stories and carols of Christmas nourish your heart, and may you share them in good spirits.

Christmas Stories

The following Christmas stories and story collections are widely available in bookstores and libraries. Explore among them, with a special eye toward stories that would be good to tell to loved ones, young or old, on a snug winter's evening.

Alcott, Louisa May. "Christmas at Orchard House" (many editions).

Andersen, Hans Christian. "The Fir Tree" (many editions).

Beilenson, Nick, ed. *A Christmas Medley*. New York: Peter Pauper, 1989.

Bolger, Dermot, ed. *Dolmen Book of Irish Christmas Stories*. New York: Dufour, 1986.

Charlton, Jim, and Shulman, Jason, ed. *Family Book of Christmas Songs and Stories*. New York: Putnam, 1991.

Christmas Treasury. New York: Sunset, 1987.

Corrin, Sara, and Corrin, Stephen, ed. *The Faber Book of Christmas Stories*. New York: Faber & Faber, 1984.

Dagliesh, Alice, ed. *Christmas*. New York: Scribners, 1962.

Dickens, Charles. "A Christmas Carol" (many editions).

Garland, Hamlin. "My First Christmas Tree" (many editions).

Garrison, Webb, ed. *A Treasury of Christmas Stories*. New York: Rutledge Hill Press, 1990.

Goode, Diane, ed. *Diane Goode's American Christmas*. New York: Dutton, 1990.

Grimm, Jacob, and Grimm, Wilhelm, ed. "The Elves and the Shoemaker" (many editions).

Harper, Wilhelmina. ed. *Merry Christmas to You*. New York: E. P. Dutton, 1965.

Haugan, Rudolph E., ed. *Christmas: An American Annual of Christmas Literature & Art*. New York: Augsburg Fortress, 1980.

Henry, O. [William Sidney Porter]. "The Gift of the Magi" (many editions).

Howells, William Dean. "Christmas Every Day" (many editions).

Johnson, Lois S., ed. *Christmas Stories 'Round the World*. New York: Rand McNally & Co., 1962.

Koppelman, Susan, ed. *May Your Days Be Merry & Bright & Other Stories by Women*. Indianapolis: Wayne State University Press, 1988.

Low, Alice, ed. *The Family Read-Aloud Christmas Treasury*. New York: Little, 1989.

Luckhardt, Mildred C. *Christmas Comes Once More*. New York: Abingdon, 1962.

MacLeod, Charlotte, ed. *Christmas Stalkings*. New York: Warner, 1992.

Maguire, Jack. *O Christmas Tree!* New York: Avon, 1992.

Morris, Frank, ed. *A Christmas Celebration: The Wanderer's Christmas Anthology*. New York: Wanderer's Press, 1983.

Pepper, Dennis, ed. *An Oxford Book of Christmas Stories*. New York: Oxford University Press, 1988.

Sechrist, Elizabeth Hough. *Christmas Everywhere*. Philadelphia: Macrae Smith, 1962.

Steffens, Lincoln. "A Miserable, Merry Christmas" (many editions).

Thomas, Dylan. "A Child's Christmas in Wales" (many editions).

Toner, Gerald H. *Lipstick Like Lindsay's & Other Christmas Stories*. New York: Pelican, 1990.

Wernecke, Herbert H., ed. *Christmas Stories from Many Lands*. Philadelphia: Westminster Press, 1962.

Williams, Ira, Jr. *The Piano Man's Christmas & Other Stories for Christmas*. New York: Abingdon, 1986.

Yolen, Jane, ed. *Hark! A Christmas Sampler*. New York: Putnam, 1991.

Christmas Carols

For advice on caroling excursions, see "Tips for Caroling," Chapter 6.

Angels We Have Heard on High

1. Angels we have heard on high,
   Sweetly singing o'er the plains,
   And the mountains in reply,
   Echoing their joyous strains,
   Gloria in excelsis Deo,
   Gloria in excelsis Deo.

2. Shepherds, why this jubilee?
   Why your joyous strains prolong?
   What the gladsome tidings be
   Which inspire your heav'nly song?
   Gloria in excelsis Deo,
   Gloria in excelsis Deo.

3. Come to Bethlehem and see
   Him whose birth the angels sing;
   Come, adore on bended knee,
   Christ the Lord, the newborn King.
   Gloria in excelsis Deo,
   Gloria in excelsis Deo.

Away in a Manger

1. Away in a manger, no crib for a bed,
   The little Lord Jesus lay down his sweet head;
   The stars in the sky looked down where he lay,
   The little Lord Jesus asleep in the hay.
2. The cattle are lowing, the poor baby wakes,
   But little Lord Jesus no crying he makes;
   I love thee, Lord Jesus! Look down from the sky,
   And stay by my cradle till morning is nigh.
3. Be near me, Lord Jesus, I ask Thee to stay
   Close by me forever, and love me, I pray;
   Bless all the dear children in thy tender care,
   And take us to heaven to live with thee, there.

Deck the Halls

1. Deck the halls with boughs of holly
   Fa la la la la, la la la la.
   'Tis the season to be jolly,
   Fa la la la la, la la la la.
   Don we now our gay apparel,
   Fa la la, la la la, la la la.
   Troll the ancient Yuletide carol,
   Fa la la la la, la la la la.
2. See the blazing Yule before us,
   Fa la la la la, la la la la.
   Strike the harp and join the chorus,
   Fa la la la la, la la la la.
   Follow me in merry measure,
   Fa la la, la la la, la la la.
   While I tell of Yuletide treasure,
   Fa la la la la, la la la la.
3. Fast away the old year passes,
   Fa la la la la, la la la la.
   Hail the new, ye lads and lasses,
   Fa la la la la, la la la la.
   Sing we joyous, all together,
   Fa la la, la la la, la la la.
   Heedless of the wind and weather,
   Fa la la la la, la la la la.

The First Noel

1. The first Noel, the angels did say
   Was to certain poor shepherds in fields as they
      lay,
   In fields where they lay keeping their sheep.
   On a cold winter's night that was so deep.
      (Refrain)
      Noel, Noel, Noel, Noel,
      Born is the King of Israel.

2. They looked up and saw a star
   Shining in the East, beyond them far;
   And to the Earth it gave great light,
   And so it continued both day and night.
      (Refrain)

3. And by the light of that same star,
   Three wise men came from country far,
   To seek for a king was their intent,
   And to follow the star wheresoever it went.
      (Refrain)

4. This star drew nigh to the northwest,
   O'er Bethlehem it took its rest,
   And there it did both stop and stay,
   Right over the place where Jesus lay.
      (Refrain)

5. Then entered in those wise men three,
   Fell reverently upon their knee,
   And offered there, in his presence,
   Both gold, and myrrh, and frankincense.
      (Refrain)

6. Then let us all with one accord
   Sing praises to our Heavenly Lord
   That hath made heaven and Earth of nought,
   And with his blood mankind hath bought.
      (Refrain)

God Rest Ye, Merry Gentlemen

1. God rest ye, merry gentlemen,
   Let nothing you dismay,
   For Christ our heavenly savior
   Was born upon this day,
   To save us all from Satan's power
   When we were gone astray,
   (Refrain)
       O tidings of comfort and joy, comfort and joy,
       O tidings of comfort and joy.

2. In Bethlehem, in Jewry,
   This blessed babe was born,
   And laid within a manger
   Upon this blessed morn,
   To which his mother Mary
   Did nothing take in scorn,
   (Refrain)

3. From God, our Heavenly Father,
   A blessed angel came,
   And unto certain shepherds
   Brought tidings of the same;
   How that in Bethlehem was born
   The son of God by name,
   (Refrain)

4. "Fear not," then said the angel,
   "Let nothing you affright.
   This day is born the savior
   Of virtue, power, and might,
   So frequently to vanquish all
   the friends of Satan quite,
   (Refrain)

5. The shepherds at those tidings
   Rejoiced much in mind,
   And left their flocks a-feeding
   In tempest, storm, and wind,
   And went to Bethlehem straightway,
   This blessed babe to find,
   (Refrain)

6. But when to Bethlehem they came,
   Whereat this infant lay,
   They found him in a manger,
   Where oxen feed on hay;
   His mother Mary kneeling,
   Unto the Lord did pray,
   (Refrain)

7. Now to the Lord sing praises,
   All ye within this place,
   And with true love and brotherhood
   Each other now embrace.
   This holy tide of Christmas
   All others doth deface,
   (Refrain)

Good King Wenceslas

1. Good King Wenceslas looked out
   On the Feast of Stephen,
   When the snow lay round about,
   Deep and crisp and even.
   Brightly shone the sun that night,
   Though the frost was cruel,
   When a poor man came in sight,
   Gath'ring winter fuel.

2. "Hither, page, and stand by me,
   If thou know'st it, telling;
   Yonder peasant, who is he?
   Where and what his dwelling?"
   "Sire, he lives a good league hence,
   Underneath the mountain,
   Right against the forest fence,
   By Saint Agnes' fountain."

3. "Bring me flesh, and bring me wine;
   Bring me pine logs hither.
   Thou and I will see him dine,
   When we bear them thither."
   Page and monarch, forth they went,
   Forth they went together,
   Through the rude wind's wild lament,
   And the bitter weather.

4. "Sire, the night is darker now,
   And the wind blows stronger;
   Fails my heart, I know not how;
   I can go no longer."
   "Mark my footsteps, my good page,
   Tread thou in them boldly.

Thou shalt find the winter's rage
Freeze thy blood less coldly."

5. In his master's steps he trod,
Where the snow lay dinted.
Heat was in the very sod
Which the saint had printed.
Therefore, Christian men, be sure,
Wealth or rank possessing,
Ye who now will bless the poor,
Shall yourselves find blessing.

Go Tell It on the Mountain

1. When I was a seeker, I sought both night and day,
   I sought the Lord to help me, and he showed me
       the way. Oh,
       (Refrain)
       Go tell it on the mountain,
       Over the hills and everywhere,
       Go tell it on the mountain,
       That Jesus Christ is born.
2. He made me a watchman upon the city wall,
   And if I am a Christian, I am the least of all. Oh,
   (Refrain)

Hark! The Herald Angels Sing

1. Hark! The herald angels sing,
   Glory to the newborn King!
   Peace on Earth, and mercy mild,
   God and sinners reconciled!
   Joyful, all ye nations, rise!
   Join the triumph of the skies!
   With th'angelic host proclaim,
   Christ is born in Bethlehem!

   (Refrain)
   Hark! The herald angels sing,
   Glory to the newborn King!

2. Christ, by highest heav'n adored,
   Christ, the everlasting Lord!
   Late in time, behold him come,
   Offspring of the virgin womb!
   Veiled in flesh the Godhead see!
   Hail th'incarnate Deity!
   Pleased as man with man to dwell,
   Jesus, our Immanuel!

   (Refrain)

3. Mild he lays his glory by,
   Born that man no more may die,
   Born to raise the sons of Earth,
   Born to give them second birth.
   Ris'n with healing in his wings,
   Light and life to all he brings!
   Hail, the son of righteousness!
   Hail the heav'nborn prince of peace!

   (Refrain)

It Came Upon a Midnight Clear

1. It came upon a midnight clear,
    That glorious song of old
    From angels bending near the Earth,
    To touch their harps of gold:
    "Peace on the Earth, good will to men,
    From heaven's all gracious King."
    The world in solemn stillness lay
    To hear the angels sing.

2. Still through the cloven skies they come,
    With peaceful wings unfurled,
    And still their heavenly music floats
    O'er all the weary world.
    Above its sad and lowly plains
    They bend on hovering wing,
    And ever o'er its Babel sounds
    The blessed angels sing.

3. O ye, beneath life's crushing load,
    Whose forms are bending low,
    Who toil along the climbing way
    With painful steps and slow,
    Look now, for glad and golden hours
    Come swiftly on the wing.
    O rest beside the weary road,
    And hear the angels sing.

4. For lo! the days are hast'ning on,
    By prophets seen of old,
    When with the ever-circling years,
    Shall come the time foretold,

When the new heaven and Earth shall own
The prince of peace, their king,
And the whole world send back the song
Which now the angels sing.

Jingle Bells

Dashing through the snow,
In a one-horse, open sleigh,
O'er the fields we go,
Laughing all the way.
Bells on Bobtail ring
Making spirits bright,
What fun it is to ride and sing
A sleighing song tonight.
Jingle bells, jingle bells, jingle all the way!
Oh, what fun it is to ride in a one-horse, open sleigh!
Jingle bells, jingle bells, jingle all the way!
Oh, what fun it is to ride in a one-horse, open sleigh!

Joy to the World!

1. Joy to the world! The Lord is come.
   Let earth receive her king.
   Let ev'ry heart prepare him room
   And heav'n and nature sing,
   And heav'n and nature sing,
   And heav'n, and heav'n, and nature sing.
2. Joy to the world! The savior reigns.
   Let men their songs employ.
   While fields and floods, rocks, hills, and plains
   Repeat the sounding joy,
   Repeat the sounding joy,
   Repeat, repeat, the sounding joy.
3. He rules the world with truth and grace,
   And makes the nations prove
   The glories of his righteousness
   And wonders of his love,
   And wonders of his love,
   And wonders, and wonders, of his love.

O, Christmas Tree!/O, Tannenbaum!

1. O, Christmas tree!
   O, Christmas tree!
   How faithful is thy foliage!
   O, Christmas tree!
   O, Christmas tree!
   How faithful is thy foliage!
   You keep your green
   And lovely glow
   In summer and in winter snow.
   O, Christmas tree!
   O, Christmas tree!
   How faithful is thy foliage!

2. O, Christmas tree!
   O, Christmas tree!
   You give us so much pleasure!
   O, Christmas tree!
   O, Christmas tree!
   You give us so much pleasure!

O, Tannenbaum!
O, Tannenbaum!
Wie treu sind deine Blatter!
O, Tannenbaum!
O, Tannenbaum!
Wie treu sind deine Blatter!
Du grunst nicht nur
Zur Sommerskeit,
Nein, auch in Winter, wenn es schnei
O, Tannenbaum!
O, Tannenbaum!
Wie treu sind deine Blatter!

O, Tannenbaum!
O, Tannenbaum!
Du kanst mir sehr gefallen!
O, Tannenbaum!
O, Tannenbaum!
Du kannst mir sehr gefallen!

At Christmastime	Wie oft hat nicht
We gaze on you	Zur Weihnachtszeit
And feel great joy	Ein Baum vond dir
That thou art true.	Mich hoch erfreut!
O, Christmas tree!	O, Tannenbaum!
O, Christmas tree!	O, Tannenbaum!
You give us so much pleasure!	Du kannst mir sehr gefallen!

O, Come, All Ye Faithful!/*Adeste, Fideles!*

1. O come, all ye faithful — Adeste, fideles,
   Joyful and triumphant, — Laeti triumphantes,
   O come ye, o come ye, — Venite, venite,
   To Bethlehem! — In Bethehem!
   Come, and behold him — Natum videte
   Born the king of angels. — Regum angelorum.
   (Refrain)

   > O come, let us adore him, — Venite, adoremus,
   > O come, let us adore him, — Venite, adoremus,
   > O come, let us adore him, — Venite, adoremus,
   > Christ the Lord! — Dominum!

2. Sing, choirs of angels, — Cantet nunc, Io
   Sing in exultation, — chorus angelorum,
   Sing, all ye citizens — Cantet nunc aula
   Of heav'n above! — Caelestium!
   Glory to God, — Gloria, gloria
   Glory in the highest! — In excelsis Deo!
   (Refrain)

3. Yea, Lord, we greet thee, — Ergo qui natus,
   born this happy morning! — Die hodierna,
   Jesus, to thee by glory giv'n. — Jesu, tibi sit gloria!
   Word of the father, — Patris aeterni
   Now in flesh appearing: — Verbum caro factum:
   (Refrain)

O, Holy Night!

1. O, holy night! The stars are brightly shining.
   It is the night of the dear savior's birth.
   Long lay the world in sin and error pining,
   Till he appeared, and the soul felt his worth.
   A thrill of hope, the weary world rejoices,
   For yonder breaks a new and glorious morn!
   Fall on your knees! O, hear the angel voices!
   O, night divine! O, night when Christ was born!
   O, night divine! O, night, O night divine!

2. Led by the light of faith serenely beaming,
   With glowing hearts by his cradle we stand.
   So, led by light of a star sweetly gleaming,
   Here came the wise men from Orient land.
   The king of kings lay thus in lowly manger,
   In all our trials, born to be our friend!
   He knows our need, to our weakness no stranger!
   Behold your king! Before the lowly bend!
   Behold your king, your king! Before him bend!

O, Little Town of Bethlehem

1. O, little town of Bethlehem,
   How still we see thee lie.
   Above thy deep and dreamless sleep
   The silent stars go by.
   Yet in thy dark streets shineth
   The everlasting light.
   The hopes and fears of all the years
   Are met in thee tonight.
2. For Christ is born of Mary,
   And gathered all above
   While mortals sleep, the angels keep
   Their watch of wond'ring love.
   O, morning stars together
   Proclaim the holy birth,
   And praises sing to God the king,
   And peace to men on Earth.
3. How silently, how silently,
   The wondrous gift is giv'n!
   So God imparts to human hearts
   The blessings of his heaven.
   No ear may hear his coming,
   But in this world of sin,
   Where meek souls will receive him still,
   The dear Christ enters in.
4. O holy Child of Bethlehem,
   Descend to us, we pray.
   Cast out our sin, and enter in,
   Be born in us today.

We hear the Christmas angels,
The great glad tidings tell.
O, come to us, abide with us,
Our Lord Immanuel!

Silent Night

1. Silent night, holy night!
   All is calm, all is bright,
   'Round yon virgin mother and child,
   Holy infant, so tender and mild;
   Sleep in heavenly peace,
   Sleep in heavenly peace!
2. Silent night, holy night!
   Shepherds quake at the sight.
   Glories stream from heaven afar,
   Heav'nly hosts sing alleluia;
   Christ the savior is born!
   Christ the savior is born!
3. Silent night, holy night!
   Son of God, love's pure light,
   Radiance beams from thy holy face,
   With the dawn of redeeming grace,
   Jesus, Lord, at thy birth,
   Jesus, Lord, at thy birth!

The Twelve Days of Christmas

1. On the first day of Christmas my true love sent
   to me
   A partridge in a pear tree.

2. On the second day of Christmas my true love
   sent to me
   Two turtle doves and *(re-sing previous gift)*

3. On the third day of Christmas my true love sent
   to me
   Three French hens, *(re-sing previous gifts)*

4. On the fourth day of Christmas my true love sent
   to me
   Four calling birds, *(re-sing previous gifts)*

5. On the fifth day of Christmas my true love sent
   to me
   Five golden rings, *(re-sing previous gifts)*

6. On the sixth day of Christmas my true love sent
   to me
   Six geese a-laying, *(re-sing previous gifts)*

7. On the seventh day of Christmas my true love
   sent to me
   Seven swans a-swimming, *(re-sing previous
   gifts)*

8. On the eighth day of Christmas my true love
   sent to me
   Eight maids a-milking, *(re-sing previous gifts)*

9. On the ninth day of Christmas my true love sent
   to me
   Nine drummers drumming, *(re-sing previous
   gifts)*

10. On the tenth day of Christmas my true love sent
    to me
    Ten pipers piping, *(re-sing previous gifts)*

11. On the eleventh day of Christmas my true love
    sent to me
    Eleven ladies dancing, *(re-sing previous gifts)*
12. On the twelfth day of Christmas my true love
    sent to me
    Twelve lords a-leaping, *(re-sing previous gifts)*

We Three Kings

1. We three kings of Orient are.
   Bearing gifts, we traverse afar,
   Field and fountain, moor and mountain,
   Following yonder star.
      (Refrain)
      O, star of wonder, star of night,
      Star with royal beauty bright,
      Westward leading, still proceeding,
      Guide us with thy perfect light!

2. *(Melchior)*
   Born a king on Bethlehem plain,
   Gold I bring to crown him again,
   King forever, ceasing never,
   Over us all to reign.
      (Refrain)

3. *(Caspar)*
   Frankincense to offer have I,
   Incense owns a Deity nigh;
   Prayer and praising all men raising,
   Worship him, God most high.
      (Refrain)

4. *(Balthazar)*
   Myrrh is mine; its bitter perfume
   Breathes a life of gathering gloom,
   Sorrowing, sighing, bleeding, dying,
   Sealed in a stone-cold tomb.
      (Refrain)

5. *(All)*
   Glorious, now, behold him arise,
   King and God and sacrifice;
   Alleluia, alleluia,
   Earth to the heav'ns replies.
   (Refrain)

What Child Is This?

1. What child is this who, laid to rest,
   On Mary's lap is sleeping,
   Whom angels greet with anthems sweet
   While shepherds watch are keeping?
   This, this is Christ the King,
   Whom shepherds guard and angels sing!
   Haste, haste to bring him laud,
   The babe, the son of Mary!

2. Why lies he in such mean estate,
   Where ox and ass are feeding?
   Good Christians, fear, for sinnners here
   The silent Word is pleading.
   Nails, spear shall pierce him through,
   The cross be borne for me, for you:
   Hail, hail, the Word made flesh,
   The babe, the son of Mary.

3. So bring him incense, gold, and myrrh,
   Come, peasant, king, to own him.
   The King of Kings salvation brings;
   Let loving hearts enthrone him.
   Raise, raise the song on high,
   The virgin sings her lullaby!
   Joy, joy, for Christ is born,
   The babe, the son of Mary!